THE SNOWSHOE BOOK

THIRD EDITION

William Osgood
and Leslie Hurley

THE STEPHEN GREENE PRESS · LEXINGTON, MASSACHUSETTS

P9-BZT-520

Third Edition

Reprinted 1985

Text copyright © 1971, 1975, 1983 by William E. Osgood and Leslie J. Hurley

Drawings by Grace A. Brigham

This book is manufactured in the United States of America. It is designed by Irving Perkins Associates and published by The Stephen Greene Press, Lexington, Massachusetts. Distributed by Viking Penguin Inc.

Library of Congress Cataloging in Publication Data

Osgood, William E., 1926–
    The snowshoe book.

    Bibliography: p.
    Includes index.
    1. Snowshoes and snowshoeing.   I. Hurley, Leslie J.
II. Title.
GV853.08   1983   796.9'2   83–14055
ISBN 0–8289–0432–4 (pbk.)

We dedicate our snowshoe book to all the folks who appreciate the winter scene: the solemn forests and the windswept fields. We hope that our work will appeal to those who have not yet known the pleasures of walking on the snow. We hope that our pleasures and happiness may become theirs.

ACKNOWLEDGMENTS |

In giving thanks to the many, many people who have helped us in the preparation of this new edition, we first of all give a generous round of applause to our wives, Thelma Osgood and Pauline Hurley, who provided the congenial environment in which to practice the writer's craft. George E. Bosworth of the United States Snowshoe Association (USSSA) has been particularly helpful with background material on snowshoe running and racing, as well as many other topics. For information about current trends in snowshoe manufacturing we thank Baird Morgan at Vermont Tubbs, Clarence S. Iverson of Iverson Snowshoes, and Roger Burgis of the Sherpa Snowshoe Co.

In Canada, we are grateful to Magella Aidans, Roméo Daoust and Claude Letarte for taking time out of their busy schedules to talk with us about current trends in Canadian snowshoeing. Ludger and Linna Müller-Wille were more than generous with assistance and kind hospitality at their home in St-Lambert, Québec. Judy Petch of Thunder Bay, Ontario, has kept us up-to-date with many interesting letters about snowshoeing and related topics.

Charles and Marilyn Racine of Craftsbury, Vermont, tipped us off to several fruitful leads for our research.

That well-known "Iron Man" of Northfield Falls, Vermont, Douglas Wiggett, has always been a source of inspiration when it comes to outdoor activities. Several people have aided us by supplying photographs and they have been given credit by the photos. The Research and Publications Committee of Norwich University in Northfield, Vermont, has been liberal with financial aid in the preparation of the book.

Finally, a special word of thanks to all who by deed or word of mouth out on the snowfields or at the research desk helped us in many significant ways.

William E. Osgood

Leslie J. Hurley

Northfield, Vermont

CONTENTS |

ACKNOWLEDGMENTS   vi

PREFACE   ix

CHAPTER 1 | **6,000 YEARS OF SNOWSHOES**   1

    Early Beginnings   Indians as Innovators   Snowshoe Clubs
    Snowshoe Hikes   Snowshoeing Today

CHAPTER 2 | **SELECTING SNOWSHOES**   17

    Snowshoe Styles   Variations on the Theme
    Snowshoe Construction   Maintenance

CHAPTER 3 | **BINDING BASICS**   34

    A Simple Combination   An Army Variation   Alaskan Favorites
    For More Heel Control

CHAPTER 4 | **CLOTHING AND SUNDRY**   45

    Clothing Principles   Supplementary Equipment   Traction Aids
    Handy Extras

CHAPTER 5 | **TIPS ON TECHNIQUE AND TRAVEL**   56

    First Steps   Moving Out Uphill   Downhill Travel
    Poles As Aids   Cross-Country Travel   Group Travel

CHAPTER 6 | **WINTER SAFETY**   71

    Survival in the Snow   Snowshoe Repair   ABC's of Avalanches
    Winter Rescue

CHAPTER 7 | **A WINTER CAMP** 92

The Toboggan Camp   Simplify!   Tents   Campfires and Stoves
Rules of the North

CHAPTER 8 | **FUN AND GAMES ON SNOWSHOES** 96

Compass Games   Fox and Geese   Dodge Ball   Potato Races
Mad Trapper

CHAPTER 9 | **SNOWSHOE RUNNING AND RACING** 100

Running Equipment   Conditioning   Organizations   Events
Sandshoeing

CHAPTER 10 | **MAKING YOUR OWN** 111

List of Tools and Equipment   The Babiche   The Frame Stock
Making the Jig   The Steamer   Fabricating the Frames
The Lacing   Lacing the Shoes   Using a Kit
"Half-hour" Snowshoes

RESOURCE LIST 137

NORTH AMERICAN SNOWSHOE MAKERS 140

INDEX 147

PREFACE |

Since the first and second editions of our book, published in 1971 and 1975, have been so well received by our readers, we feel under an obligation to provide them with up-to-date information and have tried to do so in this completely revised new third edition. We have made minor changes throughout the book to reflect new conditions. The chapter on running and racing on snowshoes has been thoroughly rewritten. We feel that this aspect of snowshoeing may become much more popular and hope that many people will come to enjoy the pleasures of snowshoe jogging, even if they do not wish to undertake the more strenuous commitment to snowshoe racing. Brand new to this edition is a chapter describing unique approaches to winter camping, such as the idea of using a toboggan camp, and the re-introduction of that ancient Athabaskan snow shelter, the *Quin-zhee*. Our list of snowshoe makers of North America has been thoroughly verified and enlarged, and we note that there is at least one commercial snowshoe maker outside of North America — in Monaco! We have been especially pleased to see that the earlier editions of our book have been translated into French and hope that further translations will help to spread the word about snowshoeing throughout all the northern and southern latitudes of the snow world.

William E. Osgood

Leslie J. Hurley

Northfield, Vermont

6,000 YEARS OF SNOWSHOES

Very old snowshoe made of branches and bark. NATIONAL MUSEUM OF CANADA

Those who have enjoyed the pleasures of slipping quietly through the snow covered forest aisles need not be reminded of the satisfactions that snowshoeing offers to all who claim an affinity with nature in winter. With this book, it is our hope to entice many new members into the ancient brotherhood of snowshoers while at the same time perhaps widening the horizons of the sport's already numerous fans.

EARLY BEGINNINGS

The use of snowshoes dates back over an incredibly long span of human history. Archeologists have been unable to date the origin of either skis or snowshoes, but the best evidence suggests that the first device to serve as a foot-extender for easier travel over the snow was originated in Central Asia about 4000 B.C. Thus the snowshoe/ski is one of the oldest inventions of man, ranking in importance with the wheel.

Without the snowshoe/ski, aboriginal peoples would not have been able to expand over, and occupy, the northern hemisphere. Once this important contribution to technology had been made, certain human groups began their

1

northward migrations which eventually enabled them to move from a central point somewhere in Asia into what are now known as Scandinavia, Siberia and the Americas.

Asia and the Americas were once joined by land at the place where the Bering Strait now separates the United States from the Soviet Union. It was then that the various predecessors of the American Indian and the Eskimo moved into the Americas. This eastward migration bridge apparently became the demarcation point between the use of snowshoes and skis. The westward moving peoples evidently favored the ski for, in the course of human history, skis became the favored means of transportation in northern Asia and Europe. Interchange between Asia and the Americas in the region of the Bering Strait declined and these two human populations developed independently each with its own culture. Interestingly enough the snowshoe became a major part of the North American cultural heritage.

Indians as Innovators

Indians, as distinguished from Eskimos, were the great innovators in snowshoe design. Indians tended to move into the forested temperate zone where snowshoes were an absolute necessity for getting around in wintertime. Eskimos, living in the polar regions, did not find snowshoes essential for they traveled mostly over sea ice or on the wind-packed snow of the tundra. Accordingly, snowshoes are not too often seen amongst Eskimo groups.

The Athapascan Indians of the Northwest and the Algonquin Indians of the Northeast as well as the powerful League of the Iroquois brought the snowshoe to the greatest peak of perfection. Starting with a basic bearpaw design, they introduced hundreds of variant patterns suited to all possible conditions. Before the horse was reintroduced to America by the Spaniards, even the Plains Indians used showshoes to hunt buffalo and it could be truly said that one common cultural characteristic of all the Indian tribes in any region where snow covered the ground in wintertime was the snowshoe.

Insofar as we know from the Norse sagas, the first white men to set foot in North America led by Leif Ericson around 1000 A.D. made no mention of snowshoes being used by the Indian groups they came upon. But there is no question that snowshoe travel was well established at that time by Indians in Labrador and on Newfoundland. This is a curious omission in the otherwise detailed sagas.

Probably the first white people to make extensive adaptation of the snowshoe were the French who began to move in and colonize the St. Lawrence River area in the 1600's. The French tended to intermingle freely with the Indians and they quickly learned how to make best use of the snowshoe in wintertime and canoe in summer. The great heroes of the French colonial period, d'Iberville, Le Moyen, Hertel de Rouville, de Nantel, and many others, were experienced snowshoers. During the prolonged French and Indian War, the struggle between French and English for dominion in North America was almost swayed

Indians hunting buffalo on snowshoes as depicted by George Catlin. PUBLIC ARCHIVES OF CANADA

Another Catlin painting shows an Indian war dance on snowshoes. PUBLIC ARCHIVES OF CANADA

An early Canadian soldier on snowshoes, from a 1722 French history. PUBLIC ARCHIVES
OF CANADA

to the side of the French by their superior tactics and by the way they, with their Indian allies, used snowshoes as a tactical aid for making lightning raids on English settlements.

English and Dutch pioneers moving into the hinterlands also made use of Indian lore and skills to maintain their settlements in the face of French opposition. In 1690 a group of French and Indians attacked a community near what is now Schenectady, New York, taking both prisoners and household goods. The settlers gathered their forces and pursued the marauders over fifty miles on snowshoes, and recovered the prisoners and stolen goods after heavy fighting. Another person who learned well from the Indians was Robert Rogers, who put his knowledge to good use as a scout for the English armies fighting on the borderlands. The famous 1758 Battle on Snowshoes near Lake George in the Adirondacks reinforced the need for military supply officers to include snowshoes as part of the logistical support for winter warfare. In the State Papers of Vermont, for example, there are several references to payments made to furnish the militia with snowshoes.

During the great westward expansion period, snowshoes were equally as important as the axe and flintlock rifle in the zones where snow lay deep throughout the winter season. Trappers, hunters, explorers and surveyors in these areas found snowshoes to be indispensable.

Both the Indians and the white men in these times usually made their own snowshoes according to the patterns which had been defined by the Indians long before the white men came to North America. The making of snowshoes was a home industry for the most part, although certain people who had a particular knack for the craft probably made some snowshoes for sale or barter.

Indian groups maintained the lead in snowshoe manufacture until very recent times and even now some of the best and least expensive snowshoes are made in Indian communities. A good example of this industry is the little village of Indian Lorette a short distance north of Quebec City where descendants of the Huron tribe still make an excellent product for sale in Canada and the United States (see the list of snowshoe manufacturers on page 140).

The Spread of the Ski

Historically then, the snowshoe was dominant in North America until sometime in the 1800's when immigrating Norwegians, Swedes, and Finns introduced the ski. The process of the cultural diffusion of the ski was slow at first. Indians and the white men who preceded the Scandinavians continued to prefer the snowshoe until the 1930's when skiing began to make its phenomenal rise as a major form of recreation. Even then, the form of skiing which took precedence was downhill sport, with some means of mechanical transport to get the skier to the top of the slope. Snowshoeing continued to be the principal means of utilitarian travel for trappers, hunters and woodsmen as well as for significant numbers of people who just liked to wander around in the winter forests for pure pleasure. It was not until the late 1960's that the use of skis for touring began to be popular in the United States and Canada.

St. George's Snowshoe Club members pose for a formal 1884 portrait, complete with their gay uniforms and mascots. MANITOBA ARCHIVES

THE SNOWSHOE CLUBS

Despite the rising popularity of other forms of winter recreation, snowshoes have certainly not been displaced. This is especially true in Canada's Province of Quebec where the use of snowshoes is firmly rooted in tradition.

One of the particularly interesting aspects of this tradition is the snowshoe club which still has a place of honor in many parishes. The origin of these clubs apparently dates back to the time when military regiments formed teams and organized snowshoe races to whet competition and encourage physical fitness. The lineage of some of these clubs dates back more than two hundred years to early French Canadian days. Later these clubs became exclusively civilian in membership and control but a certain touch of military esprit lingered on, as was evident in their continued use of drum and bugle corps, flags and banners, officers, scouts, and even mascots.

A Bit of Dash

By far the most unique aspect of these snowshoe clubs was their tendency to create colorful uniforms with brightly colored sashes and knitted tuques. In the course of time certain colors came to be identified with particular districts. For example, blue was distinctive of the area near Montreal, white around Trois Rivieres, while red was typical of Quebec itself. Usually the color was displayed on the headgear or sashes, with the latter worn over a tunic. An arrow design often ornamented the sashes. Footgear was most often the high, soft-soled moccasin. And, of course, most important were the snowshoes which were made especially lightweight to be swift for racing.

The English in the Province of Quebec likewise were fascinated by the idea of the showshoe club and, especially in the Montreal area, founded enthusiastic organizations with many members and interesting events. Apparently the most active of all these organizations was the Montreal Snow Shoe Club founded about 1840. In 1882 its vice president, Hugh W. Becket, wrote a history and record of the club with a synopsis of the racing events of other clubs. Another excellent account of this interesting period in snowshoeing history is the article entitled "Tuque Bleue" by Rosemary Lunardini in the winter 1976 issue of *The Beaver* (published by the Hudson's Bay Co.).

In addition to arranging racing meets, these clubs also had a strong social orientation centered on the idea of good fellowship. Often during the wintertime the members would gather of an evening and hike out to an inn or tavern where they would have a good supper and then hike back, arriving at a late hour. This idea of an evening outing drifted south into the United States as you will see in our description of the New England community snowshoe hikes. However, the strong club organization, with its races and uniforms, remained much more typical of the Canadian scene.

Canadian Snowshoer's Union

On the eighth of March 1907 the Canadian Snowshoer's Union was founded in the clubhouse of the Montreal Amateur Athletic Association. It aims to regulate and direct the sport of snowshoeing for about sixty member clubs located primarily in the Province of Quebec. Another major purpose of the union is to maintain the customs and traditions of snowshoeing. Clubs of the union must have at least twenty-five fully active members in order to remain in good standing. From this, one can see that there are at least 1,500 enthusiastic participants in organized snowshoeing affiliated with the Canadian Snowshoer's Union. The Union's Promotion Coordinator is Mr. R. Goudie of 44 Toulon St., Gatineau, P.Q. J8T 4V6 Canada. Phone (819) 568–5516.

Another organization which was founded about 1975 is the Quebec Federation of Snowshoers and Hikers. The headquarters is at 1415 Jarry Est., Montreal, P.Q. H2E 2Z7 Canada. Phone (514) 374–4700 ext. 450. Provincial funds help the federation develop a trail network throughout the province and encourage its use both in summer and in winter through organized activities and programs of personal development under the heading of Sentiers-Quebec.

Other Snowshoers' Organizations

In 1925 the first International Snowshoe Convention was held in Lewiston, Maine; and that same year the American Snowshoer's Union was founded. This union functions in a manner similar to the Canadian Snowshoer's Union by furnishing support and guidance to slightly over twenty member clubs located in Maine, New Hampshire, Massachusetts, and Connecticut. Antoinette Gagne is the Secretary of the American Snowshoer's Union. Her address is 260 Pleasant St., Lewiston, Maine 04240. Phone (207) 782–8167.

Binding together the community of largely French-speaking interests of the Canadian and American snowshoers' unions is the International Snowshoer's Committee whose secretary and information officer is Madame Magella Aidans. Her address is 2541 Jeanne D'Arc, Montreal, P.Q. H1W 3W1 Canada. Phone (514) 259–1183.

New on the scene is the very active United States Snowshoe Association which was organized in Corinth, New York in 1977 and now has members in twenty-seven states as well as associate members in Canada. USSSA publishes a periodic newsletter for members, assists in organizing other snowshoe clubs under its aegis, coordinates snowshoe events, sanctions amateur snowshoe competitions, records and compiles snowshoe statistics, and encourages related industry. Furthermore, it has taken a lead in introducing a variety of new and interesting snowshoe competitions to appeal to a wide range of people. Information about free membership may be obtained by writing to George E. Bosworth, United States Snowshoe Association, P.O. Box 170, R.D. 1, Corinth, New York 12822. Send your name, age, address and phone number. If

Canadian snowshoe club members gather for a moonlit night outing. CUL-VER PICTURES

you would like a snowshoe information packet, enclose certified check or money order for $3.00 to cover cost of postage and material. USSSA is a not for profit organization. USSSA has the services of a microcomputer system with a new range of services to members. There will be data base for research, printouts on request, snowshoe registration as a deterrent to theft, an equipment exchange, and other valuable programs.

Interest Elsewhere

From reading about these snowshoe organizations, one might come to the conclusion that snowshoeing is quite restricted to the northeast corner of North America. This is far from the case. One only has to look through Gene Prater's *Snow Trails: Ski and Snowshoe Routes in the Cascades,* published in 1975, to see what interest lies in the Pacific Northwest. And of course there is the race of champions held over an eighty-three-mile route from Superior to Rice Lake in Wisconsin. Then there are the Arctic Winter Games which definitely include snowshoeing events. Headquarters for the Arctic Winter Games is in Yellowknife, N.W.T., Canada. Our correspondent, Judy Petch of Thunder Bay, on the north shore of Lake Superior in Ontario, Canada, tells us of many snowshoeing events taking place in her community. So it goes—all the way from Alaska to Newfoundland—snowshoeing is enjoying a brisk renaissance.

The Olympic Dream

There is no doubt many people across North America share a common goal of hoping to see snowshoe competitions as part of the Olympic Winter Games. Snowshoeing events are not included because snowshoeing as an athletic event is not widely practiced outside of North America. There is a firm belief, however, that snowshoe competitions may soon become popular throughout the world wherever snow dominates the winter landscape. This optimism stems, in part, from the recent increase in running and racing on snowshoes here in North America. George E. Bosworth of the United States Snowshoe Association sets a proposed target date of the year 2000 when you may see snowshoe competitions in the Winter Olympic Games. It is our fervent hope that all the snowshoe organizations will be able to work together constructively to pursue this olympic dream!

SNOWSHOE HIKES

In reviewing the history of snowshoeing, we cannot ignore the community snowshoe hikes which were so popular in New England villages until the late 1920's and early 30's. Reminiscences of a group in Northfield, Vermont, provide an inside look at the workings of this once very popular form of winter recreation.

Planning and organization was quite informal. At the end of any particular winter season, a group of three would take the responsibility of getting the hikes underway as soon as the snow was deep enough the following winter, usually just after the Christmas holidays. An announcement in the local newspaper invited all those who wished to assemble at a certain hour on the village square. Beforehand, the leader and his committee would have prepared a route and arranged with a farm family for refreshments. However, information concerning the route and destination was kept secret to give a sense of novelty and suspense to the tour.

The size of these groups ranged all the way from about 30 to 100, with an average of 40 to 50 for most hikes. Old-timers and youngsters alike went along and quite often entire families turned out for the event.

In New England, snowshoers did not have special costumes for their sport. Routine outdoor clothing, chiefly heavy wool, was worn; trousers for the men and boys while the women and girls wore bloomers and sometimes skirts. A heavy mackinaw-type short coat kept the upper body warm and the headgear was a knitted tuque. Footgear was much the same then as now with high moccasins and leather-topped pacs being preferred. In Northfield the most favored style of snowshoe was the Maine model, with the Alaskan trail or pickerel snowshoe also used sometimes. Bearpaw models were apparently not much in vogue during this period. A colorful note was struck by the women who decorated their snowshoes with small tufts of red wool around the edge of the frames. Apparently this custom was adopted from Indians. Henri Vaillancourt, who has made extensive studies of Indian snowshoe designs, says that these decorations along the frames did, among certain tribes, show that the snowshoes were for women and children. However, in other tribes, the decorations adorned all snowshoes.

THE "WHIPPERS-IN"

After the group had gathered, the leader would strike out at a smart pace along the planned route. The main body would then fall in line, Indian file. Stationed at the end were two skilled men who bore the peculiar title of "whippers-in." It was their responsibility to see that no one was left behind. It was also their duty to assist any floundering ladies over fences or out of the deep snow and they usually carried along some scraps of leather and rawhide thongs should repairs to equipment become necessary. During the course of the march, rest stops would be made from time to time allowing the oldsters to catch their breath and the flirtatious to exchange a little flirtation.

After a couple of hours of snowshoe hiking in the brisk winter air, appetites would be whetted for the fresh-baked biscuits and homemade preserves, oyster stew, sandwiches, doughnuts, cider and coffee that would be waiting at the destination. Group singing filled the thirty or forty minutes between the arrival of the leader, and the most vigorous hikers, and that of the whippers-in. The farm family was reimbursed—ten cents to twenty-five cents—for the supper, depending on the situation and, no doubt, the elegance of the meal. When the hikes took place during the sugaring season it was likely that a sugar on snow party would be arranged with dill pickles and raised doughnuts to accompany the sweet maple.

SNOWSHOE SLIDING

After supper was finished the group would reassemble for the return trip which usually followed a different route and was planned to include, if at all possible, an open, steep, snow-covered bank down which all the hikers could slide, one snowshoe in front of the other. This part of the trip was a time for much fun and joking as some of the members tumbled head over heels down the slope when the toe of their snowshoes would catch in the snow and trip them up. Finally, the group would return to the point of departure about ten-thirty or eleven P.M. and break up for the walk to their respective homes and a good night's sleep.

Sometime during the course of each snowshoe hike, arrangements would be made for a committee to plan the next hike, and these people would have the responsibility of keeping the continuity so that, if conditions were right, snowshoe enthusiasts could count on weekly hikes throughout the winter.

While these community snowshoe hikes have not disappeared altogether, their popularity has been largely eroded by the multiplicity of evening activities which take up our time these days; this, plus the fact that the popularity of downhill skiing has drawn the attention of the younger members of the community snowshoe clubs away from this tradition. But that too is changing!

NEW ENGLAND FAMILY OUTING

Another type of outing very popular in New England was the family weekend breakfast hike. Especially planned so that the youngsters could tag along on their tiny snowshoes, a typical outing of this sort took place in two parts. The first stage encompassed a late Saturday hike either by moonlight or lantern light out to a dense stand of huge white pine trees where a roaring campfire would be built and a kettle of water hung to boil over the flames. Oatmeal was then stirred into the water and, after the mixture began to cook, the kettle transferred into what was known in those days as a "fireless cooker." This cooker was nothing more than a tight box insulated with sawdust or hay, with its purpose, of course, to preserve the heat so that slow cooking could continue all through the night.

Once this important task was accomplished, the embers of the campfire would be carefully banked to be in readiness for the next morning. After a last look around the campsite, the family would snowshoe back to the house — a trip of usually less than a mile, but seeming much longer to the young folks who had been made drowsy by the lateness of the hour and the flickering flames.

On Sunday morning everyone would be up early in anticipation of the outdoor breakfast and load a toboggan with eating utensils, a huge black iron frying pan, an enameled coffee pot equipped with a bail and hook so it could be hung over the fire, and the necessary bacon, sausages and eggs. With all these the family would set out again, this time over a well-packed snowshoe trail, with everyone pulling on the long rope to drag the heavily laden toboggan up the hills and across the fields. On the downgrades one person would transfer to the rear to pick up the trailing rope and hold back the toboggan from going too fast.

At the campsite the ashes would be drawn away from the coals still glowing with sufficient heat to fry the sausages, eggs and bacon. While a separate, small fire of dry pinewood was kindled to boil water for coffee, the "fireless cooker" was opened and generous servings of steaming oatmeal porridge ladled out for one and all. Usually this was eaten with thick cream and honey and, when combined with fried eggs, sausages and bacon and good coffee, made a breakfast intended to stick to your ribs. After breakfast all the eating and cooking utensils were loaded back on the toboggan for washing up later at the house.

After such a breakfast one had to do something to work it off, so the various family members would work in the pine grove trimming dead branches off the trees and carrying them by the armload back to the campsite for future fires. All of this work was done on snowshoes and was excellent practice for the young folks whose contribution in armloads of pine branches, though slight, nevertheless gave them a good sense of participation in a family effort plus the experience of walking on snowshoes while balancing a load.

With minor variations, little weekend excursions like this were a commonplace activity in many New England families. They certainly remain as vivid memories in the minds of the young participants and serve as an incentive to continue the tradition in succeeding generations. And a splendid tradition at that.

SNOWSHOEING TODAY

By far the greatest use of snowshoes today is for recreation—purely and simply to get into sympathetic oneness with the winter landscape. Man is often made anew by such a simple activity as snowshoeing—truly recreation in the finest sense of the word. Such an experience may revitalize the human spirit, often jaded by the raucous clamor of urban life and insistent demands of a complex civilization. For, as the mind and body relax, a welcome serenity quietly replaces the strained and brittle patchwork of today's conflict and disorder. If there were only an accurate measure of these satisfactions, snowshoeing would likely outrank the most potent tranquilizer and thoughtful doctors might prescribe snowshoes in place of elaborate and costly laboratory compounds.

Just as snowshoeing rewards the mind and spirit it also rewards the body, firming up muscles that often don't get enough of a workout in our rather sedentary world. At the same time it has the advantage of not being *too* demanding. Snowshoeing is a sport of moderation so far as energy expenditure is concerned. Only slightly more effort is needed to get around on snowshoes than to walk on dry ground. Of course it is possible to put heavy demands on the

Present-day snowshoe group catching their breath after a vigorous assault of Pine Mountain near Gorham, New Hampshire. PHOTO BY DICK SMITH

15

body when using snowshoes for mountaineering or in racing but, for most people, snowshoeing is a sport they can all enjoy all their lives in a quiet, undramatic—yet rewarding—way.

Other Ends

Even though a large number of people use snowshoe travel as an end in itself, many others use snowshoes as a means to further some other end. One rather common use is for winter hunting and trapping. In the deep snow belt snowshoes are an indispensable aid to tending a trap line or for getting into position for a shot at a hare flashing across a clearing. Hares themselves have evolved hind feet similar in form and function to the snowshoe which enable them to travel easily over deep snow. So it's fair to say that, more often than not, all concerned—the hunter and the hunted—use snowshoes (except the poor hounds who have to struggle through the deep snow as best they can).

Another large group in the roster of snowshoers is made up of such people as timber cruisers, foresters, surveyors, prospectors, land speculators, and electric power and telephone linemen. These people see snowshoes as primarily utilitarian implements, important in the day-to-day performance of their duties.

Then there are practical considerations where snowshoes can play a major role. For instance, we have hauled many tons of firewood by sled over winter roads using only human muscles and the ever-useful snowshoes to provide flotation and traction for the feet. Snowshoes can also replace the snowplow to some extent, for we have found that storms leaving three inches or so of light, fluffy snow can be tramped down on the driveway surface using snowshoes. Wheeled vehicles manage very well on a good, hard snow surface when temperatures remain below freezing. The colder the better.

The Snowmobile

The most recent history of the snowshoe must have some reference to the incredibly rapid rise in the popularity of the snowmobile. In looking at this phenomenon, one surely wonders if snowmobiles will completely displace the snowshoe in somewhat the same way that they replaced many dog teams throughout the North. Snowmobiles are an established fact of life, but we also see a resurgent interest in snowshoeing. In the winter of 1979–80, despite very poor snow cover, one leading snowshoe maker said he was quite optimistic about the future, partly due to some recent favorable publicity about the many rewards of snowshoeing.

Suffice it to say now that the snowshoe, almost six thousand years old, is holding its own in this incredibly complex technological age. Undoubtedly there is something in its simplicity and its closeness with nature that speaks directly to an increasing group of people who seek now to live with nature, rather than subdue it.

Selecting
Snowshoes

SNOWSHOE STYLES

Over the millenia a tremendous number, perhaps hundreds, of snowshoe models have evolved. An inventory of all the recorded styles would be an intriguing study in itself, but here we will restrict ourselves to those that are commonly available, although at the same time touching upon some of the interesting variations.

For Heavy Woods and Frequent Turning

Our experience leads us to suggest that the oval-shaped *bearpaw* snowshoe with some refinements in design is the most universally satisfactory model. The basic bearpaw style functions most effectively in heavily wooded country or in situations where making frequent turns are necessary. However, the basic style does have a few handicaps and snowshoe makers have altered its design in two different ways which have improved it considerably.

One improved model is most frequently referred to as the *otter* or *Green Mountain modified bearpaw*. While still retaining the rounded tail of the standard bearpaw, it is narrower and longer and has some up-turn added to the front. The second improved model, commonly called the *Westover modified bear paw*, retains the basic oval shape of the bearpaw, but has a stubby, squared-off tail instead of the rounded tail of the standard bearpaw. An astute observer has remarked that genuine Westover-built snowshoes are real collectors' items noted in the Northeast for outstanding workmanship and versatility of performance.

For Trails and Open Areas

In our estimation, the next most useful snowshoe style is the one used for both the *Michigan* and *Maine* models. These two models are practically synonymous; they both offer a teardrop shape with a broad and slightly upturned nose and a long and narrow tail. Probably, if one were asked to sketch a snowshoe from memory, this is the style which would appear on paper. It is a classic design, especially in the Northeast. We have also seen it described as the *Algonquin* snowshoe.

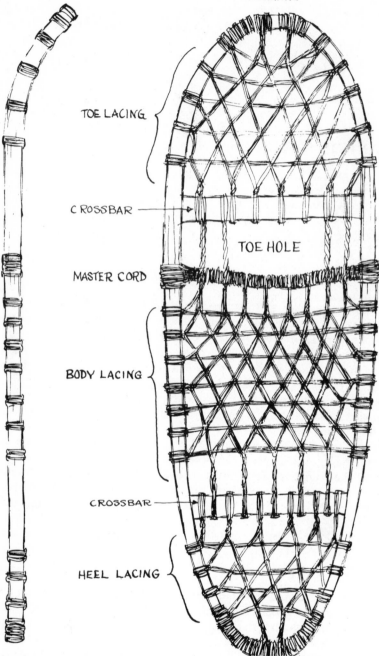

FRAME

TOE LACING

CROSSBAR

TOE HOLE

MASTER CORD

BODY LACING

CROSSBAR

HEEL LACING

Green Mountain modified bearpaw, one of the most popular snowshoe models.

For those who wish to be meticulous about distinguishing between the Maine and Michigan styles, the Maine style has a more pointed nose with slightly more upturn while the Michigan model has a rounded nose with slightly less upturn. Either of these models is good for traveling along trails or in open wooded areas. Their long tails make them track in a straight line with the way the feet are pointed. Beyond that, when the bindings are properly mounted on either the Maine or Michigan snowshoes, they are tail-heavy which is not only an advantage in keeping them on course, as noted above, but is helpful in bringing the tips out of deep snow.

The current United States and Canadian military snowshoes have been patterened after the Maine model snowshoe, although we hear that the U.S. Army, at least, is now considering the procurement of snowshoes in the Green Mountain modified bearpaw style with aluminum alloy frames and synthetic lacing. This style is both more versatile and adaptable to difficult terrain than the Maine model. We ourselves have probably used the Maine-Michigan design more extensively than any other and have been perfectly satisfied with it over gentle terrain, even though our bias still runs in favor of the modified bearpaw models.

For Deep Snow

Another popular snowshoe style now generally available is the *Alaskan*, sometimes called the *Trail, Yukon or Pickerel* snowshoe. This model is quite different in appearance from those we have discussed thus far, being particularly long and narrow, and having a most distinctively upturned toe. These snowshoes are exceptionally fine for travel in deep snow and open country. They have very little tendency to tip sidewise (which is one of the handicaps of the standard bearpaw model) and the upward flair at the toe makes it next to impossible to catch the tips in deep snow or under a crust. Heavy persons will find that the Alaskan snowshoe is best for them as its long length tends to give more support and stability. In situations requiring many short turns, this length is a decided disadvantage; likewise, in thick brush and in heavily wooded areas, the Alaskan model snowshoe is cumbersome, but for making time on the trail this snowshoe is unexcelled. This model is quite widely available in Canada and the United States through leading sports stores and mail order houses, as are the other frequently seen snowshoe models mentioned above.

Another snowshoe style to consider is the *Ojibwa*. The style of the Ojibwa is very similar to the Alaskan, and is best used in open country and deep snow. Like the Alaskan, it is long and narrow with a strong upturn at the tip. However, instead of being rounded at the tip, it is pointed—the result of its frame being made of two pieces of wood joined at tip and tail. One advantage to this type of construction is to avoid having to make the wide bend at the tip which requires special steaming techniques. Also there is an inherent advantage in a pointed tip as far as snowshoeing technique is concerned: the tip knifes through deep snow and does not load up. These snowshoes are now quite widely available, especially in Canada.

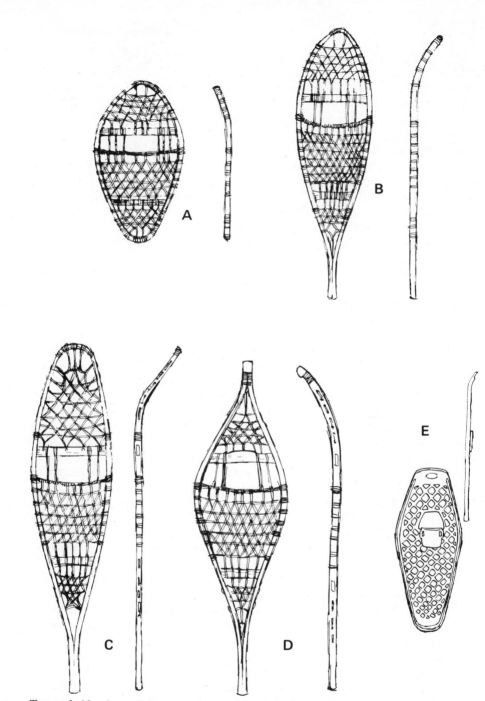

Top and side views of five snowshoe models. A is the standard bearpaw; B, the Maine or Michigan; C, the Alaskan; D, the Ojibwa; and E, a new plastic model.

For Hills and Mountains

Keep in mind that traditional snowshoe designs were evolved over centuries by Indians who used them on the level or moderate terrain of the vast subarctic forests of North America. Indians seldom traveled into real mountainous country. In the first place, the hunting and fishing wasn't so good there. In the second place, Pomola, the Evil Spirit of Mountains, lurked behind the craggy slopes, ever ready to cast rock slides and snow avalanches at hapless intruders. So it is not unreasonable to expect that present-day mountaineers would find Ojibwa or the Montagnais beavertails pretty awkward up on the steeply sloping snowfields.

Gene Prater in the Pacific Northwest was instrumental in pioneering new designs which were especially useful in coping with the deep, heavy snows and mountainous terrain of that region. Currently, several models of snowshoes share special features which make them useful in mountaineering, and they also perform quite well on the flatlands. These new styles utilize metal frames and synthetic materials for lacing and decking. They normally have some type of built-in crampon device to assure better control on the ups and downs. The binding is pivoted on a cross-rod that replaces the master cord of rawhide or synthetics. This pivot rod feature gives excellent control and eliminates the need for long tails to keep the snowshoes tracking straight. Lashings on the bindings have been remodeled to make the snowshoes easy to step in and out of. The bindings are particularly suited to the heavier mountaineering boots. Even the U.S. Army "Mickey Mouse" boots fit quickly and easily into these bindings. We have tried several of these new models and are enthusiastic about their overall performance on steep terrain. We also rate them very highly on sled hauling details, and they are certainly convenient for backpacking trips up into the hills. The "Sherpa" snowshoes have been especially popular. In addition to being particularly suited for mountaineering because of the unique "Snow Claw" built right into the binding, these "Sherpa" snowshoes are also finding wide acceptance among snowshoe racers. Vermont Tubbs has introduced their "Alum-A-Shoe" model of snowshoes that perform very well on steep slopes. Traction aid on the "Alum-A-Shoe" is built into the frame itself which, because of its special design, gives excellent edge control on traverses. "Polarpaws" are another style of innovative snowshoes especially good for use on icy snow crust. Early Winters produces their mountaineering snowshoes under the name "Northern Lights" with a special feature of being able to adjust the bindings forward or back depending on where the snowshoes are to be used, whether on steep slopes or flatland. "Northern Lights" can be purchased fully assembled or as a kit which could be assembled at home in about two hours. The Black Forest Snowshoe Co. is one of the pioneers in the field of making and selling aluminum frame snowshoes and they probably have sold more of these than anyone else both fully assembled or as a kit for home assembly. For further information about these and other snowshoe makers see our list beginning on p. 140.

The Vermont Tubbs Alum-A-Shoe. VERMONT TUBBS

Polarpaws traction aids. POLAR EQUIPMENT COMPANY

Plastic Snowshoes

Molded snowshoes cast all in one piece from special plastic resins have been on the market now for several years and have gained wide acceptance among those who carry them for emergency use, especially on snowmobile journeys out into the bush. People who only use snowshoes casually also find the plastic models quite to their liking, particularly because of their comparatively low prices; currently in the forty to fifty dollar range. Several style models are available, the most popular being some variations on the bearpaw theme. Plastic snowshoes tend to shed wet snow quite well but they are also quite slippery in these same wet, packed or icy snow conditions. A major advantage is that they are maintenance free and will stand a lot of abuse. Bindings for plastic snowshoes are generally simple, made with nylon webbing, and they are quite easy to put on and take off, however, heel control is minimal.

A lightweight and economical plastic version of the standard bearpaw snowshoe. EAST-MAN KODAK PHOTO

Variations on the Theme

As we have seen, there are commonly available a number of standard styles of snowshoes from which to choose according to your particular needs. Here, however, we would like to detail some of the interesting variations in style that have been developed for special (extraordinary) purposes over the years.

For example, what about snowshoes for horses? In an interesting woodcut dating from 1555, Olaus Magnus, the historian of the North, shows a man leading a pack horse with both leader and horse shod in peculiar round snowshoes. This is exceptional, not only for the fact that the illustration shows snowshoes on a horse, but also because it indicates that a form of snowshoe was being used in Scandinavia during the sixteenth century where, currently, snowshoes are seldom used. Our Alaskan correspondent, Joe Delia of Skwentna, also notes that horses have been trained to walk on round snowshoes for work near the mines in Alaska. Perhaps the idea for these round snowshoes for horses came from observing how well the round hooves of the caribou and reindeer adapt to travel in the snow.

The most unusual homemade snowshoes we have ever seen came from New England where Wendell H. Savery of Williamstown, Vermont, showed us one made entirely of wood. Now, snowshoes made entirely of wood boards are not too uncommon; we have seen several examples of these. The peculiar feature of Mr. Savery's snowshoe was that a third crossbar had been added to the conventional teardrop frame. This additional crossbar was set well forward and made to pivot by two pins set into holes bored through the frame. A large wooden footrest was firmly attached to this movable front crossbar. This footrest was designed to come down on the other two crossbars which were

Sixteenth century woodcut shows a mountaineer and his horse both shod in unusual round snowshoes. CULVER PICTURES

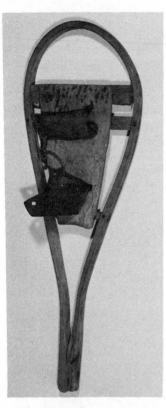

Example of an unusual type of snowshoe donated by W.H. Savery to the Northfield, Vermont, Historical Society. NORWICH UNIVERSITY PHOTO SERVICE

mortised into the frame in the usual way, using them as a platform. A second distinctive feature was the lack of any webbing at all.

Our readers may wonder how snowshoes made entirely of wood differ from skis. In the first place, the examples of wood snowshoes we have seen are perfectly flat and so, if slid forward, would dig into the snow instead of skimming on or near the surface. Secondly, these wooden snowshoes had cleats nailed crosswise on the bottom for reinforcement. These cleats would certainly prevent them from sliding as skis are intended to do. Some of these wooden snowshoes have toe holes cut through the wood, while others are solid. The latter must have been quite awkward to use because the toe hole is a distinct improvement for easy travel.

While we are on the subject of "near-skis," we should mention the combination designed in Switzerland and made by Lillywhites, Ltd., of Great Britain. This is a small snowshoe, not much larger than foot-size, laced with string and mounted directly on a short, broad ski. Apparently this hybrid never became popular, for Roger Gilman reports from Switzerland that snowshoes are still a curiosity there, although the Swiss Army has at least two models of small snowshoes in use.

The Aleuts of the Alaska Peninsula have a device for over-snow travel which is basically a ski in form and design. The frame is about ten inches wide by five feet long and is entirely covered with sealskin with the hair pointing backward.

25

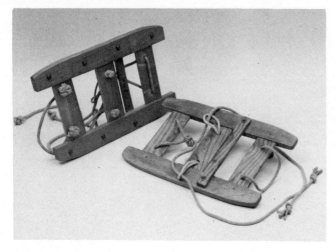

Swiss army snowshoes made entirely of wood. At left is a view of the bottom of the snowshoe and at right a view of the top. NORWICH UNIVERSITY PHOTO SERVICE

Another style of Swiss army snowshoes. NORWICH UNIVERSITY PHOTO SERVICE

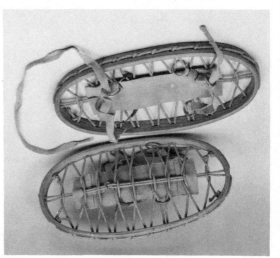

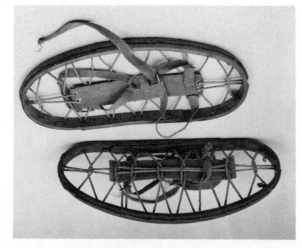

Snowshoes owned by Bill McNamara, Northfield, Vermont. Made before 1900. NORWICH UNIVERSITY PHOTO SERVICE

Eastern Cree weaving fancy beavertail snowshoes. VAILLANCOURT PHOTO

Such a snowshoe/ski would be slid along the surface of the snow and one would be prevented from slipping backwards by the slope of the hair. This, of course, is the same principle long used by skiers who attach special climbing skins to the underside of their skis for extended climbs. Joe Delia, who mentioned the Aleutian snowshoe/ski in one of his letters, said he had never seen an example of them, only heard about them from older natives.

There is now on the market a short, stubby "Bushwhacker" ski made on the principle invented ages ago by the Aleuts. It is distributed in the U.S. by Trak of Newburyport, Massachusetts, for about eighty-five dollars. However, instead of using a sealskin bottom, a plastic base is applied and imprinted with a fishscale pattern which allows the "Bushwhacker" to slide forward and prevents it from slipping backward. We have tried these skis and find them excellent, having the best qualities of both snowshoes and skis.

Also from Alaska comes news of some enormous snowshoes appropriately called "whales." These are fourteen inches wide by *seven* feet long. Joe Delia says that these monsters are absolutely essential for traveling over the heavy snows found on the southern slopes of the Alaska Range. Russ Merritt of Cohasset, Minnesota, makes a few of these seven-footers each year to his own designs. See list of snowshoe makers on p. 140.

Another snowshoe variation designed for use in the deep, light snows of Canada is sometimes referred to as the "beavertail." This has been made and used extensively by the Montagnais and Naskapi Indians living east of James Bay. The most common dimension for this style is nineteen by twenty-six inches. It is the most nearly circular of all the snowshoes we have seen except the exotic specimens recorded by Olaus Magnus. The "beavertail" is usually laced with a very fine mesh to give maximum support in soft snow.

To round out our list of off-the-beaten-track snowshoes — Swedish manufacturers now have for sale a saucer-shaped snowshoe which is short and wide. The frame, curiously enough, is made of bamboo. The lacing is provided from wide straps of rubber or Neoprene impregnated canvas. The style is apparently derived from the Norwegian "Truger," a snowshoe for emergency use and not much good for long distance travel because there is no toe hole.

SNOWSHOE CONSTRUCTION

The proper construction of conventional snowshoes is not only an interesting study but an important thing to know when one is planning to acquire a new pair of snowshoes. The following look at the steps involved in this years-old craft will give our readers an idea of what to look for.

The Frame

White ash is the best wood for snowshoe frames. It should be selected for fast growth and straight grain and should preferably be air-dried rather than kiln-dried. The air-dried wood has longer life. Nowadays, most of the frame stock is quarter-sawn, but the very best frame stock has been split from the tree in such a way that the grain is only slightly interrupted thus giving incredible strength. Only a few hand craftsmen will take the time to split out frame stock so your chances of finding this kind of material are very slight. Quarter-sawn frame stock makes up the bulk of what is used for commercially manufactured snowshoes. Look the frame over carefully and examine the grain of the wood to be sure that it runs straight and that there are no knots or other visible defects.

Also considered as part of the frame are the wooden crossbars, usually two in number. Examine the joints where the crossbars are mortised into the frame and be sure that the workmanship there is neat and tight. The edges of the crossbars and frame should be rounded to eliminate sharpness and to give a clean, smooth appearance. Holes bored through the frame and crossbars should be slightly countersunk to eliminate sharp edges that might wear into the webbing. If you are selecting snowshoes with metal frames be sure that all bends are smooth, that there are no crimps and, if the style of frame involves a joining of the ends of the frame, look over the workmanship of this joint carefully and reject any frames with ill-made joints whether welded or otherwise fastened.

The Webbing

No matter what the material used for lacing snowshoes, whether synthetic or natural, the most important point to consider is the tightness of the strands. Loose or slack webbing indicates poor workmanship and, especially in snowshoes laced with rawhide, the slackness will increase as the snowshoes get wet. Walking on snowshoes with slack webbing is rather like walking on a soggy pancake fried in lukewarm grease—an awful sensation!

The webbing, netting, filling, or lacing of snowshoes is an interesting story itself. The basic concept behind snowshoe lacing is to provide enough light, yet strong and durable, surface area to keep a person from sinking down too deeply into the snow. In addition, the lacing should be attached to the snowshoe frame in such a way as not to weaken the frame unnecessarily. Since snow comes in a multitude of forms, varying from one part of the winter to another and also in one part of the snow belt to another, one will find that the basic snowshoe designs have been refined to suit various conditions and geographical regions. Perhaps the most elaborate refinements have been in the various types of webbing or filling. For coarse, granular surfaces, sometimes called "corn" snow, or thick crusts and wind-packed surfaces, a heavy, open webbing is best. On the other hand, a fine mesh is desirable for travel in light, fluffy snows.

For most snowshoes, there are three sections to be considered as far as lacing is concerned. The first and most important section is the center—usually between the front and rear crossbars. Here is where the foot is attached and where the main weight distribution falls. Generally the materials used to lace this section are heavier and the weave more open. In some cases, though rarely, this is the only section to be filled and the front (toe) and rear (heel) sections are left open. Usually, however, the front and rear sections are filled, commonly with a lighter gauge material than that used for the main or center section. The method of attachment to the frame is different also. In most cases the lacing is attached to the center section by wrapping while, for the front and rear sections, holes are often bored through the frame to provide attachment points.

SYNTHETICS

What of the materials used for snowshoe webbings? Today almost all agree that synthetics make the best webbing. The specific synthetics in this case are a combination of nylon fabric and a heavy Neoprene coating. This form of webbing is resistant to most forms of decay, is not attractive to gnawing animals, is water repellent, and is tremendously strong. An important added feature is the fact that it does not tend to stretch when moist so that, if the snowshoes are well made and laced tightly to begin with, they will stay that way indefinitely. Another attractive feature is the fact that snow does not cling to the Neoprene coating meaning that snowshoes laced with synthetics do not load up with snow as quickly as those laced with natural materials. Also we now see an increasing use of sheet synthetics used for snowshoe decking in the place of the intricate lacing patterns which are so labor intensive.

Although this is still the subject of some discussion, most indications point to the fact that Neoprene coated lacings will last as long or longer than rawhide. As a matter of fact, the well-known snowshoe maker, Clarence Iverson of Shingleton, Michigan, says, "We find the Neoprene we use in our shoes lasts about four times longer than the rawhide lace." He adds that these synthetics do vary considerably in quality and that prospective buyers should insist on nylon reinforced Neoprene. Some Neoprene lacings, he reports, break up under the pounding of racing on hard packed courses.

RAWHIDE, TRIED AND TRUE

Rawhide, until recently, has provided most of the webbing for snowshoes. Simply defined, rawhide is the skin of some animal with the hair removed. Such a skin is not tanned in the usual sense, but first dried for preservation, then soaked in water so it can be cut into strips and made flexible for the lacing process. The rawhide shrinks in drying after the lacing is done so that a well-laced pair of snowshoes has taut webbing. Next the snowshoes are usually treated with a waterproof varnish to keep moisture from getting at the rawhide and loosening it up.

Our investigations reveal that the very best natural material for snowshoe lacing is beaver hide, but since beaver skins are more valuable with the fur on, it is a rare pair of snowshoes that is laced with beaver hide. Next in line for snowshoe webbing is ordinary cowhide taken from two-year-old steers. Caribou and reindeer hides have also been used extensively. However, these skins are not as good as cowhide because they tend to stretch more easily. Moosehides, sealskins, and bearskins have also been noted as useful for snowshoe webbing.

It may be interesting to note that these various hides when used for snowshoe lacing fall under the term *babiche* (sometimes, babbiche or bacbiche)— undoubtedly an Indian name which has been used enough by English speaking people to be generally understood in backwoods sections. We have heard snowshoe lacings referred to as "gut," but have never known of any which were actually laced with gut which, strictly speaking, would be made from the intestines of some animal rather than from its hide.

Although animals hides make up by far the bulk of natural materials used in lacing snowshoes, there are some instances where vegetable products have been used. From Yugoslavia and Czechoslovakia we have heard of shrubs being cut and trimmed for snowshoe webbing, being woven in a wickerwork fashion. And, in North America, we know of many instances where twigs and stems of bushes have been used to good advantage to get out of a tight spot.

PATTERNS

Lacing patterns generally are designed to give a woven hexagonal effect in the front, center and rear sections, but hexagonal webbing is by no means universal. In Alaska it is quite common to see a rectangular lacing pattern in the center section while the front and rear sections may be laced with a hexagonal network. Interesting variations in weaving snowshoe lacings may be seen from time to time, especially in Canada, and some of these are real collectors' items as the pattern designs are often quite complex and artistic. Henri Vaillancourt has made a detailed study of these intricate lacing patterns and uses them in some of his own handcrafted snowshoes. See list of snowshoe makers on p. 140.

Nylon cord and tape is also widely used for lacing snowshoes. This material is immensely strong in service and quite indestructible. It is particularly recommended to novice snowshoe makers, for, besides being quite easy to obtain, it is convenient to manipulate by unskilled fingers. Nylon lacing is frequently included in the popular snowshoe making kits with good reason.

Other Important Points

Be sure to check the master cord (sometimes called the toe cord). This is the heavy cord running straight across the snowshoe just below the toe hole to which bindings are attached. The master cord takes the most punishment of any part of the snowshoe so, accordingly, it should have the most attention in construction.

Another important point to consider is the size of the toe hole. When bindings are properly mounted, the ball of the foot should be just about over the master cord. This means that the front of the boot should be able to move in and out of the toe hole without rubbing on the sides or on the front crossbar. A large toe hole is especially needed by those who intend to wear heavy insulated rubber boots.

SNOWSHOE SIZE GUIDE

weight (in pounds)	size (in inches)

Bearpaw - modified (the "Westover" style)

125 — 150	12 × 34
150 — 180	13 × 35
180 — 210	14 × 35

Bearpaw - modified (the "Green Mountain" style)

| up to 200 | 10 × 36 |

Bearpaw - standard

150 — 175	14 × 30
175 — 200	15 × 30
175 — 200	13 × 33
200 — 250	14 × 36

Maine

35 — 50	9 × 30
50 — 60	10 × 36
60 — 90	11 × 40
100 — 125	12 × 42
125 — 150	12 × 48
150 — 175	13 × 48
175 — 200	14 × 48

Michigan

150 — 175	13 × 48
175 — 200	14 × 48
200 — 250	14 × 52

Alaskan

125 — 150	10 × 48
150 — 175	10 × 56
175 — 200	12 × 60

Weight is another very important consideration to keep in mind when selecting a pair of snowshoes. Our chart (see opposite) suggests the proper snowshoe dimensions for persons of different weights. Don't choose the biggest snowshoes under the impression that they will keep you on the surface no matter what the consistency of the snow. *Aim for the lightest weight possible for anything and everything to be attached to your feet* — whether it be snowshoes, socks, boots, or bindings. Keep in mind that one pound on your feet is the equivalent of five pounds on your back. There is nothing to be gained in walking around with heavy, awkward snowshoes. Choose the lightest and trimmest you can find. Your reward will be miles of pleasant excursions and a pleasant feeling of exertion at the end of a journey instead of dull exhaustion.

MAINTENANCE

Wood frame snowshoes with rawhide lacing should be given a coat of waterproof spar or the newer polyurethane varnish whenever the finish gets worn. This will help keep the rawhide from soaking up water and loosening up. Synthetic lacing (nylon/Neoprene) does not need to be varnished but it is a good idea to varnish the wooden frames from time to time. When not in use, snowshoes should be stored in a cool, dry place and hung out of reach of gnawing animals in the case of snowshoes laced with rawhide.

Binding Basics

We have tried a whole range of snowshoe bindings and will share our experience here. However, any advice offered is far from the last word and we would be glad to hear from any of our readers from their own fund of knowledge so that we can further improve this section in any editions to come.

A SIMPLE COMBINATION

The most usual binding in the northeastern United States is a simple combination of wide toe-piece and leather heel strap with a cross strap over the instep (see diagram A). The advantage of this uncomplicated binding is its cheapness and ease of manufacture. With a supply of good leather, a sharp knife and a punch almost anyone could make up a set of these bindings in an evening's time. The wide toe-piece is cut so it is narrower in the front than in the back, thus shaped to fit the toe. On flat country and on gentle slopes this binding serves the purpose, but in climbing steep grades and in traversing hillsides this binding shows its weak points. The leather tends to stretch under tension so that your foot will sometimes slip out, or, in the case of making long traverses, your heel will slew downslope at an angle to the line of travel making it extremely difficult to walk comfortably.

This binding as it is commercially made (diagram B) usually has a buckle fitted to the heel strap and should be adjusted so the buckle is on the outside just below the ankle bone. The buckles can be dispensed with in a homemade pair. The ends should be long enough so they can be crossed behind the heel and tied at the instep at the point where one would tie the laces on a pair of oxford shoes. In former times, lamp wicking was often used for this heel strap and it must be admitted that lamp wicking is easier to tie than leather. However, lamp wicking tends to freeze up and, of course, nowadays is scarcely available at all. A good substitute for lamp wicking is nylon strapping about 1/2" or 5/8" wide. We have had good success with a combination of this nylon strapping and a leather toe piece and, as we mentioned previously, this makes a very inexpensive type of binding good for most purposes except mountaineering.

AN ARMY VARIATION

A variation on this conventional style of binding was developed by the U.S. Army and came into civilian use through surplus sales. This binding (diagram

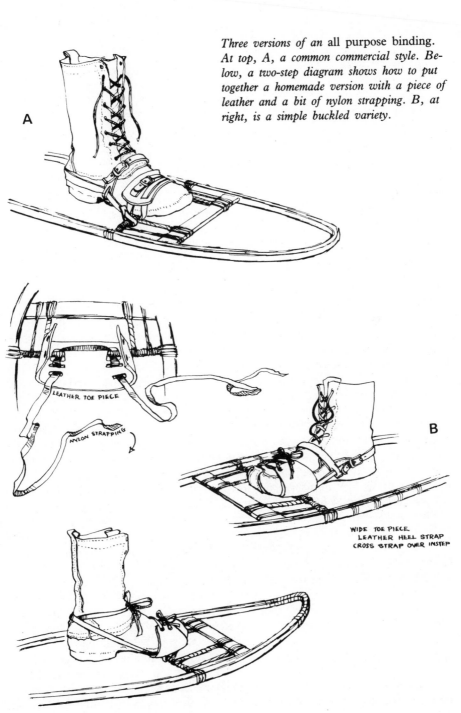

Three versions of an all purpose binding. At top, A, a common commercial style. Below, a two-step diagram shows how to put together a homemade version with a piece of leather and a bit of nylon strapping. B, at right, is a simple buckled variety.

A

LEATHER TOE PIECE

NYLON STRAPPING

B

WIDE TOE PIECE
LEATHER HEEL STRAP
CROSS STRAP OVER INSTEP

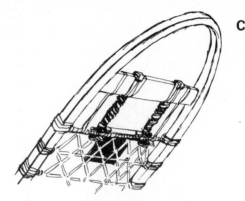

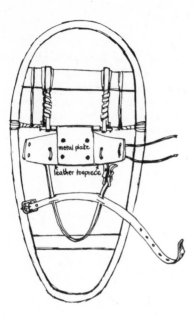

Top and bottom views of U.S. Army or Burgess Hitch snowshoe binding, *with the metal plate and leather toe-piece shown clearly from above and crust spikes from below. This binding was designed by Jack Burgess of Wallingford, Vermont.*

C) is a combination of leather and metal. A leather toe piece similar to that described above is attached to a metal plate which serves as a foot rest. A hinge pin passes through this plate at its fore-edge justs above the master (or toe) cord. The pin is secured at either end by metal straps which are bound in position by the rawhide at each side of the toe hole. The metal straps also are bent around the front crossbar so that the whole assembly becomes an integral part of the snowshoe itself. A further refinement is the addition of crust spikes or crampons located alongside the toe hole in line with the master cord. Some users have remarked that these crust spikes are a nuisance and advise that they be cut off, while others find the crust spikes quite helpful. Our experience indicates that they are worth keeping, although they may need some supplementary aids on hard crust. The remaining parts of this Army binding are conventional; being heel and instep straps as described above. (The U.S. Army binding, now called the Burgess Hitch, is available from the Snocraft Company of Scarboro, Maine.)

This Army snowshoe binding can be improved by attaching the Army flexible ski binding to the hinged metal foot plate (diagram D). The basic element in this flexible ski binding is a strip of very heavy balata-treated canvas. Newer models are made of a flexible plastic material. An integral part of the strip is a leather heel cup with strap to tighten across the instep. Also included with the flexible ski binding is a double-strapped leather toe-piece. This toe-piece has holes punched in it to match one of several sets of holes punched in the foot strip. This choice of holes allows the length of the strip to be extended to fit several sizes of boots by choosing the correct set of holes. The flexible ski binding was designed to be attached to skis with wood screws, but where the ski binding is used in combination with the hinged metal plate of the standard Army snowshoe binding, the attachment is made with copper rivets rather than with wood

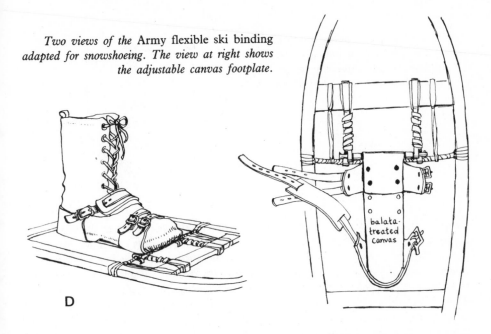

Two views of the Army flexible ski binding *adapted for snowshoeing. The view at right shows the adjustable canvas footplate.*

balata-treated canvas

D

screws. By using the flexible ski binding in combination with the standard snowshoe binding, one obtains much better lateral control of the snowshoe without sacrificing the freedom of vertical movement afforded by the hinged metal plate. The disadvantage, of course, lies in the added weight factor because the flexible ski binding weighs slightly more than the leather harness that is routine on the regular Army snowshoe binding. However, for those who like to tinker, we believe this modification is worth the effort.

Another type of binding very similar to the standard combination of wide toe-piece and leather heel strap is one on which the toe-piece folds back over the toe of the boot (diagram E). That is, the toe-piece of the binding is not open at both ends, but only at the rear where the boot can be inserted. This flap of leather or Neoprene is held in place over the toe of the boot by two straps with a buckle for adjustment. The straps also serve to attach the toe-piece to the master cord. The main advantage of this modified harness is that the boot is held from slipping forward, which is certainly a great help in going downhill.

ALASKAN FAVORITES

When we first thought about writing this book we wrote to as many people as possible to find out about different styles of snowshoes and bindings. One of our most informative replies came from Joe Delia, an Alaskan trapper from Skwentna, and in his letter he carefully described a most unique form of snowshoe binding. This binding (diagram F) was originally devised by Alaskan natives and has a long history there. It consists of a toe strap much narrower than the one described above. The heel straps are riveted or sewn to the toe

In the forward support binding, *a wide leather piece keeps the toe from sliding forward, a very helpful improvement, especially for downhill travel. It also protects the toes when digging in for a steep climb.*

strap in such a way that they fit at the sides of the boots when the boots are pushed into the toe strap. The rivets joining the heel straps to the toe strap are placed far enough apart so the ends of the toe strap can be twisted around the master cord of the snowshoes and then brought back up along the toe strap and in between the heel strap rivets, with the ends then tied together over the toe. The two trailing ends of the heel straps are tied or buckled together to form a large loop. Once the proper size of this loop is determined — based on boot size — no further adjustments need to be made to either the toe or heel straps unless wetting or tension stretches the leather.

To use this binding one merely pushes the toe under the heel strap and swings the foot up so the end of the heel strap loop is resting at the instep. Then swing the foot out and around the outside heel strap and bring the toe up and under the same heel strap and then into place through the toe strap. This process is a bit complicated to describe, but is simplicity itself in actual practice and the real beauty of this hitch is the fact that one need not bend over to attach snowshoes to one's feet. With a bit of practice a person can get into this binding in a twinkling. Likewise, it can be jettisoned equally as fast and, if one should break through thin ice, this hitch can be a lifesaver. Walking on snowshoes using this binding certainly requires more skill than with the more rigid bindings, but Mr. Delia says, "we run behind dog teams, jump logs, wade brush, cut wood with our style of harness and don't notice any lack of control."

Another slightly more complicated harness which Mr. Delia mentioned uses the "Squaw Hitch." This binding (diagram G) utilizes a separate piece of leather for the toe piece which is woven through the lacing of the snowshoe on either side of the toe hole to form a loop through which the toe can be pushed. The main binding is a long thong of rawhide tied as shown in the diagram. According to Mr. Delia, "this is the most common method of attaching the foot to the snowshoe among natives (Indian and Eskimo) and white trappers in back country Alaska." This harness and the one described just above have the advantage of great simplicity. It is surprising that they are not used extensively in the northeastern United States. It would seem that that these bindings could be used perfectly well in almost all situations — the main exception being for mountaineering which, as we have said before, requires a much more rigid binding.

F

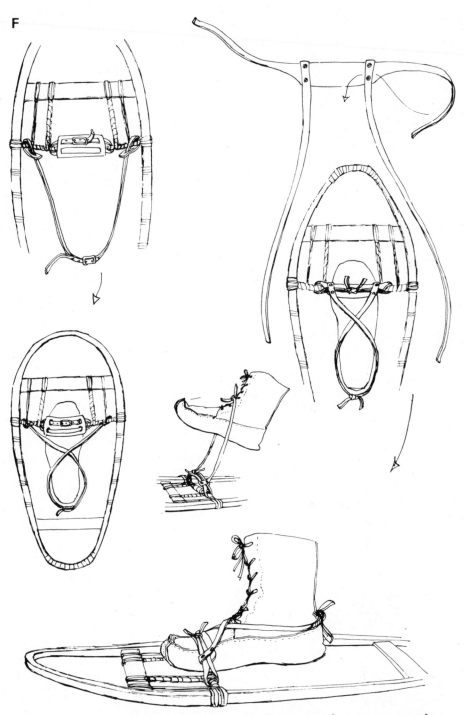

This simple native Alaskan binding *looks difficult to manage but one soon gets the knack.* SUGGESTED BY JOE DELIA

FOR MORE HEEL CONTROL

About ten years ago a special heel control snowshoe binding was developed that could be easily attached to conventional rawhide laced snowshoes. This binding did indeed provide excellent heel control. Unfortunately the hinge section was rather weak and tended to break under the wear and tear of heavy service and extremely cold temperatures. More recently we have seen the combination aluminum frame and synthetic laced or decked snowshoes become widely distributed. These newer snowshoes, designed with mountaineering in mind, have their bindings mounted on a pivot rod with nylon bushings. This arrangement is very strong. It allows easy movement of the foot up and down but virtually eliminates the sidewise slew, long the bane of hill-climbing snowshoers.

Another innovative snowshoe hitch has recently been introduced that combines a conventional cross-country ski binding with an attachment for snowshoes. This factory-mounted system from Vermont Tubbs permits the snowshoer easy in and out while also giving excellent control over a variety of terrain.

SIMPLE AND CHEAP

An old rubber inner tube from an auto or truck tire can be the source material for two other kinds of snowshoe bindings. The first, and simplest, is made by cutting off two crosswise sections from the tube to form a couple of rubber bands about half an inch wide each (diagram I). These rubber bands can then be combined with the toe straps of the snowshoes to make a quick and convenient hitch to keep the feet from slipping out of the toe straps. The handiest way to use this harness is first to slip the rubber bands over the boots up to the ankles. Then one steps into the toe straps so that the toes project through the straps. The rubber bands are then pulled forward over and then under the toes of the boots. The tension of the rubber keeps the feet from sliding back out of the toe

Modern heel control binding introduced by Sherpa. SHERPA PHOTO

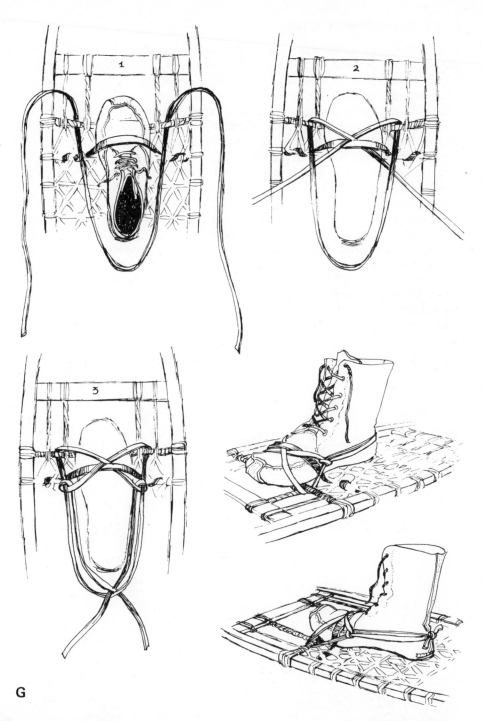

Simplicity itself — the Squaw Hitch — *another native Alaskan binding makes use of just a long leather thong.*

straps. This type of harness does not give much heel control, but it does have the advantage of simplicity and cheapness and is perfectly adequate for short trips. Another advantage is its safety, as the snowshoes can easily be kicked off in case of an emergency.

The other binding using rubber inner tubing is made by cutting out a flat section in the form of a trapezoid (diagram J). First a hole sufficiently large to push the feet through is made in the center. Then holes are punched through the corners at the wide end of the trapezoid, after reinforcing these corners with an extra layer of rubber. Rawhide is then laced through these holes onto the master cord of the snowshoe in such a way as to provide enough tension on the rubber so that the foot won't slide forward when it is in place between the rubber and the master cord. The small end of the trapezoid is then pulled up over the heel and that's all there is to it. Another simple and cheap harness. This binding could be easily crafted at home, using a pair of heavy shears to cut the old rubber inner tube and an awl to punch the holes. Lest the reader be deceived by such seeming simplicity, we should add that these bindings tend to be too loose for much downhill traveling; that is, the foot will tend to slip forward since the binding does not hold the toe firmly in position over the master cord. Another drawback to this type of binding is its reaction to cold weather. Extreme cold will make the rubber

A piece of old inner tubing makes a good heel strap for a homemade binding.

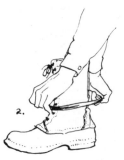

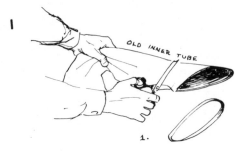

J

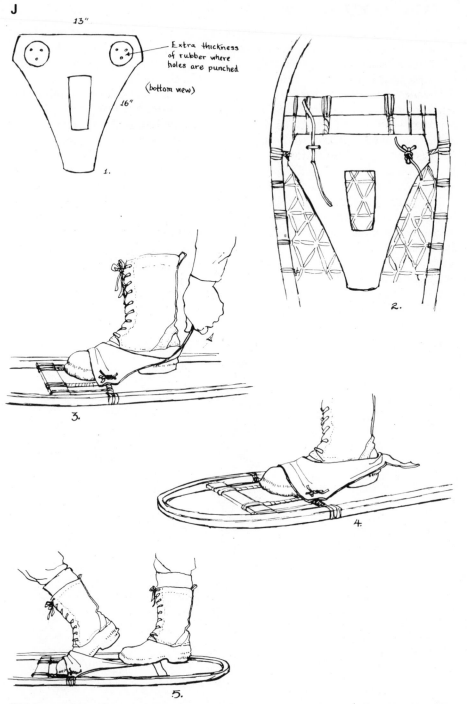

13"

Extra thickness
of rubber where
holes are punched

(bottom view)

16"

1.

2.

3.

4.

5.

Old inner tubing also can be used to make this somewhat more complicated trapezoidal
binding.

stiff and difficult to manipulate. However, for those who like to experiment, this binding is worth the time it takes to make.

To close this section on bindings, let us offer an exotic touch based on the principle of the winter boots the Laplanders make of reindeer hide. As some of our readers may know, these boots are made in such a way that the toes turn up into a point with a slight reverse curve. The boots are made this way with the functional purpose in mind to provide a simple ski binding. By slipping the toe of the boot under the toe strap of the ski, the curved toe acts to hold the boot from slipping out backwards. It seems to us that this technique would work perfectly well as a snowshoe binding. The reindeer skin for these boots is tanned with the hair on and the boots are wonderfully warm and light, especially when they are used with a lining of dried sedge in the place of socks. Of course the main disadvantage for our readers is the difficulty of getting such boots in North America. Perhaps the time will come when outlets for these boots will be established here.

CLOTHING AND SUNDRY

CLOTHING PRINCIPLES

Clothing principles for snowshoers should underline lightness, comfort, and loose fit all the way from head to toe. Make it easy for yourself to move freely and breathe deeply. What about warmth? In an active sport like snowshoeing, keeping warm is not much of a problem at all. People often overdress for snowshoeing and then get soaked with perspiration after an energetic hill climb. Then if a brisk wind comes over the brow of the hill, they really get chilled.

The best way to balance the heat budget is by layering, with the clothing arranged so that it's convenient to strip off an outer layer and stow it away in the twinkle of an eye in a day pack or fanny pack. Pullover sweaters, insulated parkas, or thick wool mackinaws are OK for the outer layer when standing around at the campsite, but for an active snowshoe hike take a look at what runners are wearing these days. Their clothing is very comfortable for snowshoeing, with perhaps that extra layer added for those who prefer to travel at a very moderate pace, or for hunters who have to stand around quite a bit waiting for game.

Footwear Ideas

Look at running shoes, too. They are wonderfully suited for snowshoeing. Their main advantage is that they are comfortable and very lightweight (remember the rule which says a pound on the foot is equal to five on the back). They are good for miles and miles of pleasant snowshoeing. Some running shoes are especially designed for winter service. The *"Gore-Tex"* (more about this later) uppers help to ease the perspiration out while blocking entry of liquid water or snow slush. But, as Mary Sinclair reminds us, keep "Gore-Tex" fabrics far, far away from destructive oils and greases. While running shoes may seem too flimsy and cold for winter wear let us remind our readers that they can be reinforced in warmth and waterproofness by adding a pair of light and flexible molded rubber overshoes. At only two and one half pounds for a medium-sized pair that reach almost to the knees it's a good bargain for the weight at current prices of about fifteen dollars a pair. Both running shoes and the rubber boots have year-round uses for outdoor minded people whether around the home, out on the trail, or at the campsite.

Another excellent type of footwear for snowshoeing is the special high top Indian mocassins that have a well-established tradition behind them. They are

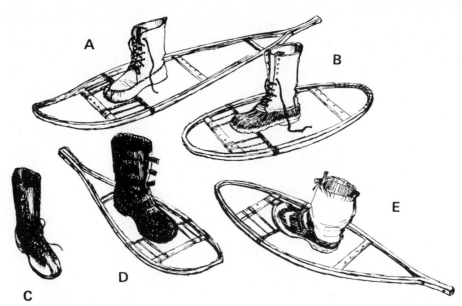

Five versions of snowshoe footgear: A, the chrome-tanned moccasin; B, the shoe pac; C, a felt boot which, when needed, can be slipped into D, an arctic; and E, a snowmobile boot.

certainly light, comfortable and warm, but unless the smooth, leather soles are covered with crepe rubber, they are terribly slippery apart from the snowshoes. The chrome-tanned leather used in many of these mocassins is quite warm in cold weather, and especially so if felt innersoles are worn. Chrome tanning doesn't make the leather waterproof, however, so in wet conditions use the mocassins with those molded rubber boots. Prices for the snowshoe mocassins range upward from twenty dollars per pair.

For people who move slowly on showshoes with lots of lengthy stops along the way, we recommend a combination of felt inner boots with waterproof outer boots. Old-time lumbermen wore felts and rubbers with great satisfaction for their daily labors in the winter woods. When it is very cold only the inner felt boots are needed — which may sound strange, but it is true. Sorel-type boots are designed with that same principle of combining a felt inner with a waterproof outer boot. These inner boots, however, are not very satisfactory to use alone as their construction is too light. A special advantage of the Sorel-type winter boot is that the inner boot usually projects slightly above the outer boot and this helps to wick out accumulated moisture.

Yet another combination of this sort is favored for snowmobiling and can also be used for snowshoeing. The felt inner boots are about the same as in the Sorel-type, but the outer boots are built with sturdy rubber bottoms and nylon fabric uppers with a drawstring or elastic band at the top to keep snow from getting into the boots. Felt and rubber combinations of whatever style are not comfortable for long hikes or rapid marches, as they tend to be much too hot and prone to raise blisters.

Cross-country ski boots and snowshoes are not an unlikely combination either. Some snowshoe bindings are especially designed to be used with the light cross-country ski boots. Boots with heels tend to be destructive to rawhide snowshoe lacings, but with modern Neoprene lacing or the full fabric decking used in mountaineering snowshoes, boot heels make hardly any impression at all. This is particularly true with the plastic snowshoes.

Another excellent type of footwear developed by Mr. L.L. Bean in 1912 and still sold by Bean's is their Maine Hunting Shoe. The good idea has been copied by many other makers of outdoor clothing. The concept of sewing a leather upper onto a rubber bottom makes a very satisfactory type of boot and it remains popular with many snowshoers, being both warm, waterproof, and comfortable to wear.

In the past few winters we have been especially interested in experimenting with the lightest types of footwear possible for snowshoeing and find that just wearing socks alone works very well for moderate type excursions in soft, dry snow at temperatures in the range of fifteen to twenty degrees below zero (F.). We wear three pairs of socks; light, medium, and heavy wool. Best for the heavy outer pair are those that are hand knit from wool spun "in the grease." Retention of lanolin in the wool fibers spun this way makes these socks very warm and remarkably waterproof.

Of course snowshoeing mountaineers need something much more rugged in the line of footwear. For extreme conditions of heavily crusted snow or ice and very cold temperatures a special double layer boot has been developed which is very expensive but probably worth its cost of about two hundred dollars a pair for serious mountaineers. The stiff sole prevents discomforts caused by snow balling up under the feet and bindings can really be cinched up to the degree required for climbing steep slopes. Also the toes of these boots are sturdy enough to stand the gaff of kicking thousands of steps without transmitting too much of the impact to the feet.

The low-cut running shoes and cross-country ski racing boots need to be reinforced against snow infiltration when you are out breaking trail in deep snow. Gaiters make an even more lightweight alternative to the molded rubber boots mentioned above; however, they are not so helpful in the case of real wet snow, where the rubber boots are far superior.

You are probably wondering why we spend so much time discussing various types of footwear. It is because feet are the weak link in systems of keeping warm. Moreover they take a good deal of physical stress during any active sport. It just makes good sense to give your feet the best treatment possible.

Next to the Skin

We are very partial to the new synthetic fabrics used for winter underwear. The great advantage of these new fabrics is that they conserve body heat while allowing perspiration to pass on through. They also have a sleek feel about them next to the skin. Pure wool is next best for winter underwear, but that fabric gives many people the itch. One way of getting around this handicap is to combine wool with cotton in layers so the cotton is next to the skin and the wool is on the outside. Some folks like the fishnet style underwear. The coarse, open mesh of this fabric helps to allow perspiration to evaporate before it has a chance to soak the other clothing. But whatever the fabric used for the underwear, be sure to get it in two parts; a top and a bottom. Union suits with drop seats are just too much of a nuisance and discomfort out there in the windy woods.

Outer Garments

As we mentioned earlier, the running clothes that have been developed in the past few years serve well for snowshoeing. A specially good feature about them is their smooth finish, which sheds snow easily. Running clothes provide for every comfort except warmth and for this you will need to add such things as the bib-type warmup pants with zippers down the sides. If you keep vital organs in the trunk of the body warm, your blood will circulate readily to extremities like hands and feet. An insulated vest filled with goose down or one of the newer synthetic fiberfills is just the ticket for this important task. Get the vest with the long tail which will help to keep that important kidney region warm and cozy.

A loose-fitting wool shirt is good to wear over your underclothing. Be sure that the shirt has a couple of good-sized pockets with button-down flaps to carry notebook and pencil, compass and whistle, among other things.

Finally, to cover the upper body as the outermost garment a good parka or anorak is indispensable. This should be of windproof, water-repellent material, cut rather full and with an attached hood.

That hood is really essential to keep snow from cascading down your neck as you pass under snow-laden branches. A hood helps to keep the wind from chilling the head and neck regions as well. A drawstring will keep the hood snugly fitted to the face. Pullover parkas are a nuisance to put on and take off, and they have the added disadvantage that you cannot open them up somewhat when you begin to feel overheated. We definitely advise that the parka have a good zipper right up the middle. Some of these zippers work from both top and bottom and this is another aid in adjusting the heat budget. Pockets on the front of the parka are useful for stowing away odds and ends which should be conveniently at hand. All pockets should be zippered and, if a good long tab on the zipper is not provided, a short length of string or thong will be a most helpful addition.

At one point fashion designers thought that the "Wet Look" should be an *in* thing. Fortunately it didn't last long for those slippery outer garments cascaded too many people to a resounding crash at the foot of steep slopes. We mention this as a caution to those who might follow absurd fashion trends to the detriment of their continued enjoyment of outdoor activity.

Headgear

Traditionally the snowshoer's headgear has been the knitted tuque (pronounced to͞ok). The tuque is of Canadian origin made with colorful woolen yarn and topped with a tassel. It is warm and light and is excellent for all kinds of winter sports. Its only disadvantage is the lack of a visor wide enough to shade the eyes from bright sunshine, so for sunny days we like to have a visored cap to wear.

For Warm Hands

A pair of cheap, light cotton gloves with knitted wristlets is about all that is needed when out on a vigorous snowshoe march on a day of moderate winter temperatures and calm air. When it is really sub-zero, though, and the wind is snaking snow plumes in amongst the snowshoe tracks, then it's time to be wearing double mittens, the inner pair being of good knit wool. Ragg type is fine but perhaps even better are mittens that have been treated to the Austrian boiled wool process. This tightens up the knit considerably and makes exceptionally warm mittens. These are sold under a trade name of Dachstein or Edelweiss and are well worth the extra expense for those who spend a lot of time outdoors. The outer shell can be made of a tightly-woven cloth with leather palm and thumb and gauntlet reaching up onto the forearm, and held closed with an elastic band to keep snow and wind out. For exceptionally severe conditions and for winter camping, carry an extra pair of mittens tucked right into your waistband where they will be warm and dry whenever needed.

Trade names like PolarGuard, Hollofil, Gore-Tex, etc. have special inference for outdoor people in that they extend the comfort range of their clothing and gear in one way or another. What about Gore-Tex? This is a thin membrane made by stretching the resin from which Teflon is made. This film has billions of tiny holes to the square inch which allows water vapor (perspiration, for example) to pass through but which blocks the entry of liquids (rain, for example). Fabrics made with Gore-Tex have an amazing number of applications for winter travellers. Here is just one example. Conventional fabric gaiters work

Coureur de bois outfitted for a cold day of hunting on snowshoes.

just fine to keep snow off the lower leg and from sifting into shoes or boots, but they can cause perspiration buildup to an uncomfortable degree. Gaiters made with Gore-Tex are more perspiration permeable and more comfortable in the long run (pun intended!). PolarGuard is another miracle synthetic that has almost as much insulating value as prime goose down but is much more resistant to wetting. It has special applications to such things as sleeping bags and outer garments. We have found that the catalogues of the best outdoor supply houses are an excellent source of information about these and other new materials.

SUPPLEMENTARY EQUIPMENT

Snowshoes in themselves when equipped with good harnesses are complete so there isn't much to say about supplementary equipment, but there are some things worth mentioning which can make travel on snowshoes easier under certain conditions.

TRACTION AIDS

There comes a time when snowshoes act too much like skis to the discomfiture of their owners. Sloping terrain could mean trouble for snowshoers. This is where traction aids come in handy. One older method of coping with this problem is winding short lengths of manila (not slippery plastic) rope in a spiral fashion around the snowshoe frames; each length is tied off to the webbing. This is similar to the "Ruff-lock" technique which has been long practiced by Indian snowshoers. In their case, instead of using rope, they wound the frame with heavy rawhide.

If you should find yourself out on a slippery crust with none of these things, it is possible to break off a few tree branches to weave through the lacing of the snowshoes to increase your traction. This technique should be practiced with care so as not to damage the lacing: it's only for use as a last resort.

If you do have a pocket knife and a few lengths of rawhide thong, a somewhat better emergency crampon can be whittled out of a tree branch. Cut the branch long enough to span the width of the snowshoe at the widest part and lash the branch crosswise of the snowshoe at each edge. It will help if the twigs on the branch are left projecting slightly from what will be the underside of this temporary crampon; then, if the surface for the upper side is stripped flat and whittled smooth at the points where it will be lashed to the frame, this will help hold your emergency crampon in place.

Another form of expedient crampon can be improvised by putting several wood screws through the upper crossbar, leaving the points long enough to act as crust spikes. We are told by Joe Delia that this technique has sometimes been used in Alaska quite effectively.

Some people use aluminum angle plates riveted to a piece of leather, which in turn is lashed to the webbing of the snowshoes just behind the master cord in the center section. A single strip of this angle stock about four inches long by

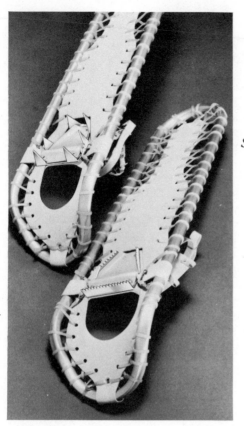

Sherpa traction aids. SHERPA PHOTO

three quarters or one inch wide is good. This strip is put in position crosswise of the snowshoe and so placed acts to keep the snowshoe from sliding forwards and backwards. A further refinement would be to add a section of aluminum stock of the same size placed at right angles to the first to form a letter T. This somewhat more elaborate sort of crampon would then help to prevent sidewise slippage. A crampon of this sort could be carried along as supplementary equipment in the pack and put on and taken off as required.

Research and development people at the Sherpa Snowshoe Co. have put a good deal of thought into traction aids and have come up with a device they call the "Snow-Claw" which is an integral part of the binding. There are two types of "Snow-Claw" currently available. The conventional model is designed for semi-severe conditions and it has serrated teeth cut into three sides of the under part of the binding just where most of the weight is concentrated. For more extreme conditions they have introduced the "Tucker-Claw" named after Dick Tucker of the Appalachian Mountain Club. This traction aid features six triangular teeth, each 1½" long for positive gripping. As the foot rotates on the built-in pivot rod, the "Snow-Claw" grips and releases with each step, with maximum grip coming just when it is needed. Another excellent feature of either type of claw is the snow guard built into the underside. This sheet of very

51

tough synthetic material helps to keep snow from balling up in the claw itself. The "Snow-Claw" idea does indeed give very good traction just where it is needed.

Walter L. Gregory of 8 Wall Avenue in Valhalla, New York, 10595, makes and sells a special snowshoe crampon which can be easily put on or taken off as required. Other types of snowshoe crampons are available from outdoor supply houses; some to be attached to the front crossbar, and others to the outsides of the frames to prevent lateral slippage.

People who use their snowshoes frequently on sloping snowfields or for hauling loads by sled prefer to have their traction aid built right into the design so it is always there when needed. An early model of this type is the Burgess Hitch described on pp. 36–7 and sold today by the Snocraft Co. of Scarborough, Maine, 04074. This binding can be attached permanently to practically any type of snowshoe. The Burgess Hitch features crust spikes which project below the underside of the snowshoe webbing.

Another excellent form of traction aid which we have tried recently is attached right onto the frame of the Tubbs "Alum-A-Shoe." This device gives the snowshoer a remarkable feeling of security on steep slopes whether climbing straight up, traversing, or descending.

Traction aid on *"Polarpaws"* is first-class. A unique crampon design featuring front points is built right into the binding. Gives a real feeling of security on steep, crusty snowfields.

An ice axe made more useful with the attachment of a ski pole basket. NORWICH UNIVERSITY PHOTO SERVICE

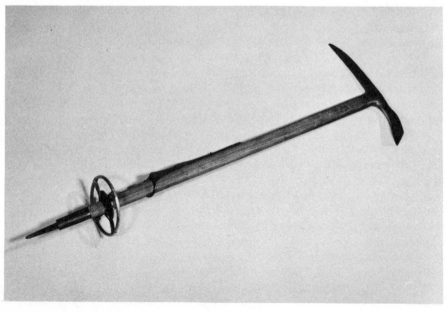

Poles

As we shall see in our section on how to walk on snowshoes, ski poles are handy things to carry while snowshoeing. If not a pair of ski poles, at least one makes a handy walking staff. Choose poles with shafts long enough to reach to the armpits when the points are resting on a hard surface like a floor. When they can be obtained the older poles with larger diameter baskets are to be preferred as the larger baskets give better flotation in soft snow. We often wind the pole shafts with tape at regular intervals so that the pole when inverted and thrust into the snow can act as a measuring instrument.

Ice Axe

In snowshoe mountaineering an ice axe is perhaps to be preferred over ski poles, but in order to be most useful the ice axe should be fitted with a ski pole basket (see illustration). With a little remodeling the standard basket can be adapted to fit the larger shaft of an ice axe. However this remodeling is done, keep in mind the fact that the basket should be fitted to the ice axe so that it can be conveniently put on and taken off. Such baskets are easily obtainable from mountaineering supply houses. Obviously the ski pole basket would be a hindrance when the ice axe is to be used as it was intended. The ice axe can save you from a long slide down a steep and slippery slope so in high country the ice axe is a much better companion than ski poles.

Winter Staff

We have also been experimenting with a device we call the winter staff which can serve a number of purposes. The idea first came from seeing a drawing of an ancient implement made and used by the reindeer-herding Sami of northern Scandinavia. Since they were skiers, they used the pointed end of the staff as a kind of rudder to help in steering and also for braking. The other end was carved into the shape of a shovel which they used around the campsite and to help the reindeer dig for the tasty lichens under the snow.

In our modification of this old idea, we put a steel chisel at one end so we can use it for cutting through ice. The other end we shave down so it will fit the socket of one of those aluminum snow shovels that is listed in mountaineering supply catalogues. The best type of shovel to use with the winter staff is the one that has a slip ring on the socket that can be used for tightening up or for removal. Unless the winter staff is actually being used for shovelling snow, we carry the shovel part on the tobaggan or in the pack. Then — to make the winter staff even more helpful — we use one of those removable ski pole baskets that were designed specifically to be used with ice axes.

When one of these baskets is fitted over the chisel-pointed end it serves as a good snowshoeing aid. In order for the winter staff to be really useful as an ice chisel it has to have a more substantial shaft than the conventional ski pole, so

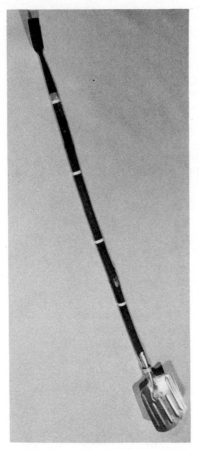

The winter staff. NORWICH UNIVERSITY PHOTO
SERVICE

we use an ash wood handle of the type made for long-handled shovels. This
length, by the way, is just about right for the winter staff. We also carve narrow
grooves in the handle so we can use it for a measure. We have been quite pleased
with this modern application of an ancient implement and hope our readers will
find it equally useful.

Handy Extras

We should also take note of a few other practical aids for snowshoers to carry
along. These items are suggested elsewhere in the book as well, but they bear
repeating. First and foremost is a good pocket knife equipped with a leather
punch. Next, any snowshoer should always have at hand some lengths of
rawhide thong or good nylon cord. Almost any field repairs can be carried out
with a knife and thongs, but some also like to have a few short strips of ⅛-by-1
inch strap aluminum to use as splints in the repair of broken snowshoe frames.
Soft wire or tape is good to use to hold the splint in place. A map and compass,
and the ability to use both, are needed when traveling in unfamiliar country. A

54

plastic police whistle is a good signaling device if you need to call for help. Don't forget to have matches in your pocket; the waterproofed wooden stick matches are by far the best for getting a fire started. And be sure to consult our chapter on winter safety for further tips for safe and happy travel in the winter woods and snowfields.

TIPS ON TECHNIQUE
AND TRAVEL

Ask an old-timer how he learned to use snowshoes and he will likely reply, "B'gosh, I dunno, it seems as though it sort of came naturally." Here, in fact, is the great advantage snowshoes have, for the technique of traveling on them is practically as simple as walking on bare ground. No long training period is required and the novice becomes confident on snowshoes in a matter of minutes. The important thing to remember is that walking on snowshoes is like a normal walking gait on a hard surface with only slight variations.

FIRST STEPS

If at all possible the beginner should learn with the aid of an experienced snowshoer on snow which the latter has prepared by tramping out a nice wide track. This serves two purposes for, while the instructor is tramping down the track, the beginner can observe how his teacher is handling the snowshoes. We recommend that the novice use the modified bearpaw of the Green Mountain or Westover design to begin with and that, at least at first, he or she use a pair of poles to help maintain balance and give a sense of security. Just before making the first step, the pole should be set out ahead and planted firmly in the snow. If, for example, the left foot is to be the first to move, the right hand pole should be planted out ahead, and a bit to the right, of the line of travel. The reason for doing this is to ensure two stable balancing points while one foot or the other is in motion. After a few sorties using this technique, the learner will find that it is no longer necessary to use the poles between each step and that only one pole is enough, except perhaps for steep ascents when the second pole will be most helpful.

Cardinal Rule

The cardinal rule of snowshoeing technique is to remember to pick up the foot to be moved ahead *over* the edge of the stationary foot and to move this foot far enough *ahead* so it won't encumber the stationary foot. Obviously one cannot walk when one foot is holding the other down. Contrary to what might be expected, this mode of walking does not require one to keep the feet wide apart in awkward positions. A normal walking position is quite in order only remembering not to step on the edges of the snowshoes. With these few tips

A beginning snowshoer taking her first steps across a snowy Vermont meadow. She already seems to have mastered the cardinal rule. ROBERT GEORGE PHOTO

firmly in mind a novice quickly gains confidence on a well-packed track moving over level terrain.

After a student has gained this confidence and has achieved a sense of balance, he should move out ahead into the deep snow and get the feel of what it is like to break track. At this point it is important to remember to shorten the steps and keep the tips of the snowshoes from getting loaded with snow. By planting the snowshoe into the soft snow heel first, one can avoid this pitfall and keep the tip unencumbered.

Likely somewhere along the way the beginner will take his first spill into the soft, deep snow and wonder how on earth he will ever get back on his feet again. Here the pole will come in handy for, if one can touch bottom so to speak, the pole can be used as a vertical prop. Then, once the snowshoes are in position the snowshoer can raise himself back on his feet. However, when the snow is so light, fluffy and deep that the pole cannot be used as a vertical prop, it can be laid horizontally on the snow and, grasped at mid-point, still serve its purpose very well.

Of course we highly recommend that mutual aid be extended in these embarrassing moments and that the fortunate snowshoer still standing lend a hand to his beleaguered companion. Before attempting to get up, no matter how aided, the snowshoer should be sure to work the snowshoes into a position flat on the snow and, in the event that the fall took place on a slope, place the snowshoes in a position horizontally across the pitch of the slope. Trees and bushes are also invaluable aids to assist one in getting upright again after a fall. As a last resort, if the snowshoes seem hopelessly snarled and the snow bottomless, the bindings can be unhitched, the snowshoes taken off and set in a good position to use as a platform to get back on your feet again. Don't thrash around needlessly. We should all take a tip from oxen who lie quietly while their drivers arrange for them to get back on their feet, unlike horses who often get panic stricken after a fall in the deep snow.

MOVING OUT UPHILL

Until now we have been describing the beginning stages of learning to snowhoe. Once a person has learned to walk easily over flat or gently rolling countryside either on a prepared track or in deep snow, and has become familiar with how to get back on his feet after a fall, he is ready to try ascents and descents. On a rather gentle slope one can climb straight up using the same technique as for flatland travel, but as the slope becomes steeper there are several pointers that can be applied. On a moderately sloping hillside the herringbone step can be used successfully. This step is made by toeing out so that the snowshoes form a slight angle to the pitch of the slope. It is not a very comfortable step to maintain for long and we recommend it only for short climbs on slopes of moderate degree. Another climbing technique is called "walking on your toes." In this technique the front of the foot is pushed

Two snowshoers moving out uphill make use of a rolling gait and step turn on their traverse.

through the toe hole of the snowshoes and dug in for a hard scrabble up the slope.

Points on Traversing

For longer, steeper climbs the best technique is the traverse. On a traverse, the climbers make diagonal tracks across the face of the slope. Thus one decreases the steepness while increasing the distance traveled. On a steep slope of wide expanse each traverse can be rather long. For steep and narrow slopes the traverses will correspondingly have to be shorter zigzags. There are two important things to learn about traversing. First, while crossing a slope, one must master the technique of edging the snowshoes so that they will rest horizontally when planted in position. Otherwise the snowshoer's ankles will soon tire and trouble with bindings will follow. The other point concerns the matter of making the turns at the end of each traverse.

Edging

Edging snowshoes is not as easy as edging skis because of the added width of the snowshoes. Thus, in order to learn edging technique more easily, the novice should, if at all possible, wear the narrower style of snowshoe such as the modified bearpaw, trail or Alaska shoe. Then, crossing a slope, he should swing the heel over to the inside edge of each snowshoe and tramp down firmly at each step. On a slope of moderate degree one can create a snowshoe track allowing both left and right feet to be approximately level just by stamping the uphill snowshoe in with more pressure. However, as the slope becomes steeper, a separate upper and lower terrace may be necessary.

On such steep traverses one pole, or a pair of poles, can be invaluable aids to help maintain balance and to serve as a pivot point in making *step turns* around at the end of each traverse. Another useful aid when climbing on snowshoes is the ice axe—a standard piece of equipment with mountaineers. In snowshoeing across steep snowfields or on a slope with an icy crust (having taken avalanche hazards into consideration first of all) the ice axe is by far the best aid to carry for it can be used to arrest a long and perhaps dangerous slide to the bottom of the slope, whereas a pole is nowhere nearly as effective in such a situation. As we saw in the chapter on equipment, when using the ice axe in soft, deep snow—as is most likely on snowshoe excursions—it pays to modify it by adding a ski pole basket to the shaft of the ice axe at about four inches from the spike tip.

Turning Techniques

The simplest turning technique can perhaps best be described by using the face of a clock for comparison. Suppose one is traveling on a traverse in the direction of ten o'clock and wants to change direction toward two o'clock. The change of direction is accomplished by placing the snowshoes in sequence, first right and then left, around in a clockwise motion. The tails of the snowshoes move least of all while the tips cover the most distance, similar to the hands of a clock. The simplest and easiest of all turns to master is called a *step turn* and as one becomes proficient at it he can make a rather sharp change of direction with only one step.

Should one need to make a sharper turn in order to go more directly back the way one came, the best way to accomplish this is with a *kick turn*—the same turn that skiers use and done the same way. Merely pick up one snowshoe or the other and turn it one hundred and eighty degrees. Settle this snowshoe firmly in place, then bring the other up and around beside it. It's as simple as that, but practice a few of these kick turns on a level, packed surface before attempting them on deep snow. Poles are very useful to help maintain balance when practicing kick turns.

Body Movement

Most snowshoe travel takes place over a surface cover of either new soft powder snow or semi-compacted old snow—both of which allow each snowshoe to sink into the snow to some extent at each step. On such snow surfaces you will find that a very slight pause at the end of each step allows the snow to coagulate. This pause, when combined with an added downward moment of force, causes subtle changes to take place in the snow structure. The changes are such that each succeeding step will be made from a firmer base than would be the case if one tried to step lightly hoping to avoid sinking in so far. Another body movement that adds to the ease of snowshoeing is a somewhat

Three styles of downhill technique: A, leaning slightly backwards; B, using cord to keep from becoming mired in deep snow; and C, the easy, if damp, way.

exaggerated shifting of weight from side to side with each step. It is almost, but not quite, a lurching step and amounts to a rolling gait that is quite characteristic of woodsmen and is particularly useful in walking on snowshoes. But take heart, these movements seem to come almost naturally after traveling on snowshoes for a short time.

DOWNHILL TRAVEL

Travel downhill on snowshoes provides the ultimate test of bindings. The weight of the traveler tends to push his toe farther into the toe piece and often, if the toe strap isn't tight enough, the toe will slide under the cross piece and send him headlong into a face-first spill. It is best to judge the slope ahead carefully and select the technique best suited to the snow cover and the pitch. Generally, if the slope is not too steep, one can lean back a bit holding back the full weight and putting pressure on the tails first. This technique will get the snowshoer

61

safely down moderate slopes. If the snow is firm and the pitch steep enough for sliding, then place one shoe directly ahead of the other and sit on the rear shoe and slide down. This is easy when wearing shoes with a generously upturned toe.

The pole or staff can be used as a rudder or brake if the going demands it. When using the poles as a brake, place them together one basket over the other for added strength and control. Be careful about where you put your weight, if too high above the snow it may break the pole. Using the poles as a brake or rudder is ineffective if placed on the shoe itself, no matter how hard one pushes, or if the basket of the ski pole is overlapping on the shoe instead of in the snow completely.

Should you come to a modest drop-off you may be tempted to jump. Go ahead. You will fast learn that the tails will hit the snow first and drop straight in while you will probably drop straight forward or backward but in both cases horizontally. Should you seriously want to jump while wearing snowshoes, tie the heel down to the webbing; you can then land in a reasonably stable position. It is worth a practice or two certainly.

POLES AS AIDS

As we have seen, poles are helpful aids to snowshoes going both uphill and down. There are two other functions they serve we should mention. One is as an aid in backing up. As you can imagine, this maneuver is next to impossible when wearing bearpaws and absolutely impossible with Algonquins or Alaskas without some aid to push the toe of the snowshoe down so that the tail can be raised high enough to get it up out of the snow backwards. A pole can be used to hold the toe down just enough to do this.

Another use for poles is as an aid in carrying the snowshoes. Place the snowshoes sole to sole and merely slip the handgrips of the poles through the toe

Making use of ski poles to back out of a difficult spot.

holes of the snowshoes. Pick up the poles as a pair and hoist the snowshoes on the poles to your shoulder. The baskets on the poles will keep the snowshoes from sliding off backwards. Of course an ice axe can be used in the same way.

Using poles as a pair is very helpful on steep climbs but as a rule only one pole is needed on most excursions. Even then, it is not always used as a walking staff but can be carried horizontally at the balance point or put over the shoulder. But take care when handling poles. They have sharp points and can cause painful puncture wounds. And remember that the ice axe is triply dangerous in this regard.

CROSS-COUNTRY TRAVEL

Once these basic techniques have been learned, the time has come to start out on some longer trips in small groups. Although we know a trapper or woodsman will often make extended solo journeys of long distances and seldom get into trouble, we strongly urge that snowshoe trips be made in small groups. This is a significant safety precaution, on top of which the pleasant companionship is an important consideration. While two people can manage nicely for short trips of an hour or so, we recommend four as the ideal number for longer excursions taking up the better part of a day or more. Then, if perchance there is an accident, one person can remain with the injured member while the other two go for help.

Trail Breaking

When any group is out in untracked snow, it goes without saying that the function of trailbreaker must be rotated from time to time, and frequently when the group is making a sharp ascent. There is no need for one person to assume the entire toilsome burden, even when the party is made up of a combination of expert snowshoers and beginners. After one person has had a stint at trail breaking he should step to the side and let the next in line take over. The former trailbreaker should wait until the rest of the party passes by and then take up a position at the rear of the group. The person directly behind the trailbreaker can also serve a useful function by not following precisely in the tracks of the leader, but by overlapping the leader's steps and thereby helping to create a smooth corridor in the snow for the rest to use.

As our readers will assume from what we have said above, traveling in Indian-file procession is standard procedure for snowshoers. However, when walking in Indian file, it is important to remember to keep a suitable interval so that one is not stepping on the tails of the snowshoes of the person in front. This seems to be a difficult lesson for some people to learn; perhaps the following trick for an exasperated snowshoer to play on the person who regularly treads on the tails of snowshoers will help. While passing under the snow-laden branches of a spruce or fir tree, give the branches a quick snap and jump from beneath to let the cold snow cascade down over the "tail-treader." All in good fun of course, for we'd hate to be accused of sowing seeds of dissension in what would otherwise be a happy party. One bath of cold snow should be enough reminder that it is only courteous to keep a polite interval open. Traveling Indian file makes it difficult to carry on a conversation up and down the line—all the more reason to take frequent breaks to examine some interesting tracks in the snow or to speculate on the age of some giant old tree.

Traveling side by side on snowshoes, although wasteful of energy, does sometimes serve a useful purpose by creating a wide track which might later be used for cross-country skiing or for dragging a sled or for helping get a snowmobile out of a tight spot. If traveling side by side is for the specific purpose of making a wide track it is best done by not walking directly abreast, but by having the second man (third, fourth, etc., as the case may be) walk just slightly behind and to the side of the leader so that the tracks overlap at the same time as width is being added.

Near Trees

In traveling under trees and near the trunks of them be extra careful of exposed bare branches in the snow especially if on a slope. Wood on wood is slippery and often the branch is icy. Also the bole of the tree may prove to have air-pocketed snow around it and let you down. People have been caught in a tree top thinking it was just a small tree or bush sticking up through the snow—a very dangerous position if alone.

Gullies and Ravines

In our discussion of snowshoe travel thus far we have assumed a relatively smooth snow surface. But while snow does tend to smooth out a lot of the rough spots and make for easier traveling, there will still be gullies to cross and other small irregularities of the terrain. In walking over this kind of country take care not to put weight on snowshoes that are only supported at the tips and tails. Snowshoes were not designed by bridge engineers and, while a well-made pair will take an amazing amount of abuse, there is no need to put them to the ultimate test and run the hazard of a broken snowshoe. Bridging the snowshoes over gullies or getting the webbing snagged up in brush and dead limbs is to be avoided whenever and wherever by taking any extra steps required.

The gullies mentioned above are not the same as small ravines and brook valleys which of course must be crossed from time to time. In regions of deep snowfall, snowshoers may follow an established hiking trail provided with suitable footbridges only to find that the bridges are so piled with snow that getting across on snowshoes involves a balancing act on a narrow ridge. In such a case it may be worth the extra time to push some of the snow off or, if wearing the short bearpaw snowshoes, one can, if careful, walk across by putting one directly in front of the other. No one should tempt fate, however, and try to put on a sideshow tightrope act for the benefit of his companions. He might have to be hauled up wet and shivering from a fall into an icy torrent; or, even worse, end up with a broken limb.

Over Ice

Brooks and streams bring to mind the subject of ice and how best to travel over frozen surfaces. Good, sound ice will support an enormous amount of weight and many winter roads are built to take advantage of good routes over frozen lakes and along ice-covered streams. Where these roads and trails have been laid out and marked by people who know their business, they can be used with no fear until the spring thaws begin.

However, in most cases one will not have the benefit of such carefully marked winter ice roads so it will not be amiss to note a few of the hazards to be considered before setting out over snow-covered ice. A party of four traveling Indian file should have a minimum of two inches of good ice under the snow before venturing forth and should maintain an interval of fifteen to twenty feet between persons. Beware of gray spots on the otherwise white surface as these gray spots are sure indicators of places where the water is only thinly frozen because of warm water welling up to the surface from springs in the bottom of the lake. Also give wide berth to points where streams flow into a pond as these places are also often poorly frozen. Traveling over river ice is much more hazardous than over lake ice as moving water freezes very irregularly if it freezes at all, and often a snow bridge will form up over moving water to camouflage a danger point.

It is only with a certain amount of trepidation that we suggest the possibility of travel over ice at all, knowing full well the hazards involved. But men always have and always will use ice roads, so it would be foolish of us not to consider them and ways to travel safely over them. Just keep these extra hazards clearly in mind and be especially alert to the many dangers involved. Actually, the snow that does accumulate on large ice-covered bodies of water is quite apt to be hard and wind packed, thereby making the use of snowshoes unnecessary. The smaller, forest-rimmed ponds are the ones which usually collect enough snow to make snowshoes an important means of transportation over them.

For those who may be making frequent trips out on the ice under varying conditions, the so-called Siwash binding (see the Joe Delia binding on page 39) is the safest to use because the snowshoes can be quickly kicked off if one does have the misfortune to break through the ice. When in doubt about the safety of ice travel, loosen your bindings before you cross. Loosen them enough so you can step out of them both instantly without having to bend down and use your hands. In fact, we recommend practicing this maneuver before crossing the ice. Another safety practice is to spread your group farther apart, as in avalanche territory. A coil of rope ready at hand and/or a long, slim pole carried by each traveler should be standard equipment for over-ice travel to help in rescue operations. And, of course, the rule of traveling in a group is especially applicable for journeys over ice.

Another Extreme

The other extreme from ice, or snow that is hard packed or with an unbreakable crust, is the very soft, light, and fluffy snow blanket on which snowshoes don't seem to be of any help at all in keeping afloat. At least they seem of no help until one tries to wallow through such snow without them. If you must travel under such conditions, try hitching a small section of light cord to the toe of each snowshoe — using the cord to pull the tip out of the mess whenever it becomes embedded. This same aid is also useful in the snow conditions often encountered near the end of winter when the snow has softened to such a degree that the snowshoes sink in too deeply to maneuver.

GROUP TRAVEL

As snowshoeing is again becoming more and more popular, more and more young people are joining in. Many Scout groups, 4-H groups, and hiking clubs are recognizing that snowmobiles and trail bikes are fine in their place but that they do not replace the satisfaction of "doing it myself" on my own two feet — no mechanical aids needed. We would like to offer a few words of encouragement and advice to these young snowshoers and their leaders.

The Sounds of Silence

To the young snowshoer on his or her first trip into the delightful and mysterious white stillness of the winter woods, it may come as a surprise to find signs of animal life there. But it is reassuring to see that their summer animal friends abound in winter as well. The proof is the countless number of tracks in the snow — as well as the deer yard signs. These tracks, many of which the

Deer tracks in the snow are fun to watch for.

youngsters may not recognize initially, seem to bond the young snowshoe traveler closer to nature.

So much has been written of nature and wildlife in the spring, summer, and fall, that some may be inclined to feel that all nature sleeps through the long, cold winters. It doesn't take many trips through snow-covered woods and fields to realize that this is far from true. While some animals hibernate, others lead very active lives.

The habits of the deer are especially interesting. These warm blooded animals often spend very tough winters, as their tracks when they "yard-up" testify. Their yards are usually found where the brush and coniferous trees are thick and offer some protection and feed, and are characterized by narrow, hard-beaten paths criss-crossing each other in the snow. The bark and tips of the branches of the trees around these yards will be missing as high up as a deer can reach by rearing up on its hind legs, and tufts of fur will be spotted clinging to the brush. From there, many runs lead to other favorite feeding areas. These paths are so heavily trodden that one can walk on them without snowshoes. Deer will quickly utilize any path made in the snow, be it by snowmobile, skier, or snowshoer, when it has hardened enough to keep them from sinking all the way to the ground. One only has to go back over his tracks a few days later to see.

Other things to watch for in the winter woods are the disappearing tracks of the field mice and shrews — tracks they make as they gleefully pop in and out of myriad tunnels they burrow to form an under-snow city as complex as man's. Then, too, there is the grouse. This bird often flies straight into a soft-snow drift to get itself completely covered with snow for a safe night's sleep, the lack of tracks helping to keep it undiscovered and the insulating properties of the snow cover serving as a warm blanket.

Not all signs of life in the snow-covered woods are quite so still, and we should warn any spring snowshoers traveling in rocky, ledgy, mountain country

that any sign of bear dens should be a warning to retreat. A mother bear in spring, especially with cubs, is anything but friendly and can travel faster on her snowshoe-wide feet than any snowshoer.

And so the youngster—as the adult before him—finds that the still woods are not still at all. The wind whistles through the pines; the tree trunks rub together, producing eerie protesting sounds. There is the crack of a tree splitting in the cold, the whish of a tree bough springing free after losing its load of snow.

For the young traveler on snowshoes and in the woods for the first time, just to fall down while attempting to back up on his shoes is an experience. How deep the snow is. How dependent he is on his snowshoes. To be able to travel on them at all is a wonder. Looking at his own tell-tale tracks leading from the distance right to himself fills him with the reassuring thought that, though in the wild, he is not lost and can always follow his own tracks back out. The young snowshoe traveler glows, reciting his adventures as though they had never happened to anyone else before. What a wonderful feeling this is. He long remembers his trip.

The Leader

While individual youngsters will no doubt hack around on their snowshoes on their own or with pals, any group snowshoeing endeavor for youngsters must

Bobcat, on the right, and red fox, at left, with their respective prints.

have a leader. Winter travel in snow and cold off the highway requires more care and consideration than summertime travel, and young people should have a qualified adult along, someone to assume the ultimate responsibility as well as enjoy the challenge and fun that all share. A true leader must have certain characteristics. Knowledge and experience, while necessary, can be acquired, but integrity, an inherent consideration for others, and a willingness to work harder than anyone else in the group are essential ingredients. A leader must have the judgment to know when to turn back, how hard to push to reach a safe place in the storm, an awareness of fatigue in the party—the real as against the feigned illness of a lazybones. Almost as important is the leader's ability to place his charges in a column of compatibility, his choice of a strong dependable whipper-in whom no one, repeat NO ONE, gets behind, and his resistance to the temptation to take unknown short cuts when time seems important but when safety should come first.

When no vital decisions have to be made, a leader's willingness to consult with his group and share his knowledge develops group entity and the feeling of participation. Sharing his plans, route, and reasons will be of definite value for future leaders when it's their turn and time to take over. Intelligent direction and division of trail-breaking tasks by the leader will help produce instant confidence within the group. This sharing of the burden and fun of breaking trail is important.

These characteristics and principles of good leadership are old-fashioned, perhaps, but tried and true principles which will never be computerized or supplanted. They will always be up-to-date in an ever-changing world, albeit a shrinking one, as far as wilderness areas go.

Size and Safety

Groups for snowshoe travel needn't be large but should have at least four members, five if its members are still young enough to require a leader. As a rule, youngsters should be at least high school age to be on their own and even then only if they are resourceful, properly equipped, and safety conscious. A group of fifteen or twenty should have sub-leaders and the trip should be carefully planned to the last detail so that the law of averages—that something unpleasant will happen to someone—does not prevail.

The benefits of group trips with young people between the ages of ten and twenty are many. Much can be gained from day trips and even more from travel that may include an overnight stay, sheltered either in cabins, lean-tos, tents, or snow pit shelters. Such experiences help young people find out who they are and how they stack up against their peers. They usually evaluate each other quite truthfully and at the same time gain an awareness of their dependence on each other, on their leader, and on each person's contribution to the group's well-being.

Gaining confidence in one's own abilities is of immeasurable value to a youngster, and the feeling engendered of kinship with others and with one's pioneering forebears, however distant, is enriching and soul satisfying. We believe that young people's groups, where weather permits, would do well to consider snowshoe tripping as a frequent activity and should work toward acquiring enough shoes so that their club or group could enjoy this activity to the utmost.

WINTER SAFETY

Travel on snowshoes in the winter snow and cold is wonderfully invigorating and a marvelous relaxation, but it is not without its dangers. Snowshoers should be prepared to cope with emergencies — whether they be a broken snowshoe, an unexpected bivouac, or a possible encounter with an avalanche.

The need for emergency repairs in the field must be considered routine. They should be planned for as simply, carefully, and confidently as is food and water. Any leader — Scout, 4-H, mountaineer, snowmobile, or whatever — would be remiss and grossly negligent if not prepared to make repairs to snowshoers or their equipment and should be well briefed in this whole area before going into the field. There is no serviceman or wrecker out in the winter boondocks.

SURVIVAL IN THE SNOW

Any snowshoer going any distance into the winter woods or snowfields should plan to carry the proper emergency equipment with him. This should include a first aid belt, map and compass, flashlight, waterproof matches or fire starters, as well as survival rations, and snowshoe repair kit.

True safety in the snow, as elsewhere, begins with prior planning. We do urge beginners especially not to start out without giving serious study to winter camping and hiking. We encourage them to check their libraries and book stores for good material on outdoor living in the winter. This material will stress leadership qualities, proficiency in map reading and compass use, common

Improvised emergency snowshoe using branches and twigs.

sense in reading weather signs and using forecasts, and the standard practice of asking the natives about the terrain to be encountered. It will also stress that the people at home base be advised of the plans, which should include where the cars will be parked, expected time of return, contingency plans, and alternate routes, etc.

Short hikes as shakedown cruises are heartily recommended; then longer trips. A winter practice campout in the backyard is not without merit. These efforts are all very worthwhile as the penalties for mistakes in the winter wilderness are apt to be severe.

Snowshoe Repair

To be properly prepared to make emergency snowshoe repairs in the field, the first step is to put together an adequate repair kit. The following is a good beginning: 1) wire, strong but pliable (copper or picture-hanging is fine); 2) rawhide lacings and thongs; 3) a jackknife; 4) a fishline or ⅛" nylon cord, about 100 feet wouldn't be too long (if traveling in avalanche country, an avalanche cord might do); 5) a pair of lightweight pliers; 6) a roll of adhesive tape or electrical friction tape.

Something Out of Nothing

The repair of broken snowshoes is not too difficult and has been discussed previously. But to replace destroyed or lost shoes, or to fashion emergency shoes where no shoes existed, is another matter. First, inventory the equipment at hand. Perhaps a pack frame, especially the packboard type, could be converted into a passable snowshoe. A simple snowshoe can be made from strong, straight green branches carefully notched and lashed. (See illustration on previous page.) The shape can be triangular or rectangular. It can be covered with regular cloth or ground cloth stretched as tightly as possible (sometimes something good has to be sacrificed). Smaller evergreen branches can be woven into the frame for support; using these same branches as a base, a harness can be improvised by lacing a strip of rawhide or thong, shoe lace,or ⅛" baling wire, or whatever you have into a figure eight pattern around the branches and the foot and fastened securely.

As a last resort when no great distance is involved, fir or other coniferous branches can be lashed to the foot to serve as a shoe. The need for possible renewal of this type emergency shoe might make back-packing some extra branches a good idea if the trip still ahead will take you out of the right timber terrain. One other possibility is to try this arrangement: two people on three snowshoes. Simply tie one snowshoer's right foot and another's left to a single snowshoe.

Any extra time spent in deliberate and careful attention to making and strengthening emergency shoes will pay off in the end. Patience is a virtue too often ignored. Any leader — or individual snowshoer for that matter — should include in his routine planning ample allowance for unscheduled stops and bivouacs for repairs to either equipment or person.

Survival Rations

A variety of emergency or survival rations are packaged in many forms. The work done on food for use in space has contributed much to this field as have the stories of survival in the arctic long ago. Several firms now put up very compact emergency kits. Chuck Wagon Foods of Newton, Massachusetts, to name one, puts out a kit consisting of compressed cereal bars, a starch jelly bar, non-melting chocolate bar, salt, single-edge razor blade, bandaids, wax-dipped matches, monofilament line, fish hooks, a piece of 12-by 18-inch heavy duty aluminum, and a survival booklet, all in a waterproofed, nonsinkable package only 4-½ by 2-½ by 1-½ inches. Just reading the contents is inspiration enough not to get lost or in serious trouble. A pocket-sized plastic bag full of GORP (Good Old Raisins and Peanuts) is a good survival ration, but you must resist the temptation to eat it before it is really needed.

Much lightweight survival-type food can be found in most supermarket food stores. Lipton's, Borden's and Knorr's all make a variety of dehydrated foods that can be bought and kept to be used for emergencies only. They have a long shelf life, take little space and are very lightweight. Beef Stroganoff, vegetable dinners, chicken dinners, cheese, ham and macaroni dishes, and the many varieties of soups are only a few. Bouillon cubes should be a part of any survival kit as they are a good supply of salt, which is often needed to help alleviate fatigue and muscle cramps. Dehydrated casseroles to which only a cup of water need be added are available in enough varieties and well-known brands to suit all tastes. Food bars that taste like candy and have no artificial preservatives abound in calories but are light in weight and perfect for trail munching as well as emergency food reserve.

The Edible Wild

However, if the winter traveler should find himself lost in the deep snow and cold, he should take heart. Even in the deep woods there are edible foodstuffs at hand. The chief task is to convince himself that he can survive, or to "psych" himself up, to use the modern term. One of our friends, Don Jennings, who is an adviser to the Vermont State Police Mountain Rescue Team, suggests that the first step is to get hungry — that takes care of the fussy palate. Then look for anything that the birds are eating; one can usually eat what they eat (try a small amount first). Of course it might be better to catch and eat the bird. This is not as dumb an idea as it may sound. The spruce partridge, or "fool bird," of the northern forests can often be knocked off a limb with a club. Porcupines are also comparatively easy to catch, and their livers are a gourmet treat. Other good emergency edibles are the nuts and seeds of the pine cones, the yellow tips of the new year's growth on the pine branches; the tips of spruce needles. One can use the tops of the cat-o'-nine tails found in frozen swampy areas. Dig down and get the roots too. Boil this then pound it up to make a gruel. Wild apples can be cooked. Lichen scraped from rocks can be simmered, steamed and pounded into gruel. It abounds in food value if not in taste.

To be sure of these emergency provisions, go hungry the first day and then try a little at night. If you are OK the next morning, then go ahead and fill up. A warning though — sometimes this type of sustenance is constipating, sometimes it definitely isn't. Be that as it may, the snow traveler has a good chance to survive in the wild if he can stay dry and protect himself. He has the most necessary ingredient — water, or a form of it. It alone can sustain life without food longer by far than food without water.

First Aid Measures

First aid measures are the same in the winter woods and snows as elsewhere, although the time factor involved in getting expert medical help must be considered and of course one should always be on the alert to protect one's own safety and that of one's friends when traveling off the beaten track in the winter.

Training in first aid is essential for anyone considering such travel and a knowledge of the effects of cold upon injuries and sickness should be a part of this training. Dr. Marlin B. Kreider's aticle, "Death from the Cold," is excellent source material. (First published June, 1960 in *Appalachia* magazine, reprints of this article can be obtained by writing to the Appalachian Mountain Club, 5 Joy Street, Boston, Massachusetts.) Assimilating this information is a must for all off-the-road travelers.

Hypothermia is the condition of a person who suffers from over exposure to the cold or to cold-wet conditions. Simply stated, it is a lowering of the body's core temperature below the normal 98.6 degrees. It is not to be confused with frostbite, which is a freezing of the flesh.

The visible physical danger signs are as follows: First the pores of the skin constrict, slowing down the body's heat loss by radiation through the skin. This shows up as goose bumps, accompanied by a restricted flow of blood to the peripheral areas of the body. The skin shows a slight blue color. The body still loses much more heat by direct conduction, especially if wet; by convection if exposed to the wind, and to evaporation if sweating. This heat loss still can and does go through the skin even though the pores are closed up tight.

Next, the body's defense mechanism goes into action, the involuntary muscles begin to quiver, and shivering takes place. This should make the victim aware that he should take steps to keep warm. If conditions do not improve and the body heat loss is not stopped, violent and uncontrolled shivering will follow, the teeth will chatter, and the skin will show an increased blue color. The functions of the brain, which is now being denied its usual flow of blood, will slow down. Mental fatigue, indifference, apathy and a lack of comprehension will become evident as the body's core temperature drops to the low nineties.

As the body's defense mechanism desperately tries to protect the vital organs with a normal temperature of 98.6 degrees, it further reduces the flow of blood, and respiration is decreased. As less and less warm blood flows to the brain, the victim goes into semiconsciousness. Movement becomes almost impossible. At the extremities of the arms and legs the temperature may be only 50 degrees and in the shoulder, neck, and head it may be 75 degrees; yet in the heart it may still be 98 degrees.

The control center of the brain, which sends the signals that regulate respiration and heart beat, becomes erratic and ceases to function properly. Fibrillation of the heart is noticeable, the lungs fill with liquid, and death usually results when the body's core temperature is reduced to about 74 degrees.

There are two distinct but different conditions under which hypothermia may take place:

1. Acute or rapid onset. This may develop in a matter of minutes as when a person falls overboard into icy water, resulting in the immediate chilling of the entire body. Body heat loss in cold water can be up to twenty-five times faster than in cold air.
2. Chronic, or slow-developing hypothermia. This may take hours or even days. When the body loses heat faster than it produces it, even though it be over a sustained period, the signs of chilling, fatigue, dehydration and shivering, as mentioned above, occur although their stages of progression may be longer in developing.

The treatment for acute hypothermia differs from that of the slow-developing type. It is important, therefore, to recognize the difference between the two.

Those suffering from rapid or acute hypothermia must be warmed immediately with the trunk being warmed first. This is because if attempts are made to warm the entire body at once, cold blood from the extremities will be returned to the heart, chancing that the heart will go into fibrillation and cardiac arrest. This is often referred to as "after drop." Therefore, it is essential to protect the victim at the outset from further heat loss and to rewarm the trunk to well above the critical temperature.

Fluids are not recommended for victims who do not respond to treatment or are unconscious. They are of minimal importance even when the patient is conscious, and there is always a chance that fluids will be drawn into the lungs. However, if a person is in the early shivering stages of hypothermia, sipping hot sweet fluids may be of value.

Chronic or slow-developing hypothermia victims who are beyond the shivering stages should be rushed to professional medical help since blood chemistry changes may have already taken place. It is usually better to leave them cold while at the same time preventing them from becoming colder. But if medical care is not available, the same steps as in cases of acute hypothermia should be followed. In addition, mouth-to-mouth breathing should also be used to provide warm moist air for the victim.

A blanket to warm the body is of little value, inasmuch as moist heat is required to warm victims of hypothermia. A good emergency measure is to remove the victim's clothing and put him in a sleeping bag or under a blanket with another nude person beside him. The warm moist heat from the nude body will transfer to the patient. The patient's head should also be covered, since as much as 70 percent of heat loss can be by way of the head.

A final warning: warm the trunk first.

A core temperature of 81 degrees is about the lowest a victim of hypothermia can have and survive. Try also to keep the patient conscious by talking to him; his chances of survival and complete recovery will be fifty percent. But when victims lose consciousness, the chances of survival are less than that.

All mentioned treatment for hypothermia victims applies to isolated conditions when it is impossible to transport the victim to medical facilities within a matter of hours.

The rule of thumb in the latest studies seems to be get the victim to hospital facilities. Do not try to warm the victim first.

The blood chemistry and vital signs need to be monitored before deciding which life-saving measures should be used. If the victim is rational and can walk — let him. If he is incoherent or comatose, transport him as is.

A declaration of death cannot be made upon a cold body. It is even a law in some Scandinavian countries that the body must be warmed, or allowed to warm up gradually, before a diagnosis of death can be made.

Snow travelers should watch each other for signs of frostbite when the wind is high and the temperature low. Freezing or frostbite shouldn't happen, but if it does, it's very evident. Frozen flesh when thawing out is very painful. Be alerted, however, that frostbite once thawed should not be used, bent or rubbed, but treated as a wound against infection and brought to medical attention. If it can't be treated immediately, it should be quickly thawed out and kept quiet until it can. "Frostbite," Bradford Washburn's excellent article which first appeared in the June, 1963 issue of the *American Alpine Journal*, is available from the Museum of Science, Science Park, Boston, Massachusetts, 02114. Phone (617) 742-1410.

Let us mention here a couple of other problems that snowshoers may encounter from time to time with suggestions about ways to alleviate them. The first of these is the *snowshoe ailment,* more commonly known by its French name of *mal de raquette.* This is a crippling cramping of the muscles in the lower legs and thighs which is serious enough to lay a person up for days. Another version of this is a painful inflammation of the Achilles tendon at the heel. This inflammation is most usually the result of a heel strap in the snowshoe binding which is too tight. The binding illustrated on p. 35 circumvents this problem by having the heel strap placed lower where it will not chafe the Achilles tendon. In the case where leg muscles get cramped, this is purely and simply a case of poor conditioning or overexertion. Despite best intentions, all of us get into this type of situation from time to time. Salt helps to relieve the cramps but rest is the best medicine of all. The second problem may occur when snow is soft and sticky and tends to ball up underfoot, causing great, unpleasant lumps which could even fracture small bones in the foot. This so-called march fracture sometimes afflicted infantry soldiers who marched long distances with heavy packs — another case of overexertion. Where snow balling underfoot is a problem, stiff-soled boots will help protect the feet. The Sherpa snowshoe binding also has a design feature built in which minimizes that snow balling handicap.

ABC'S OF AVALANCHES

The snow traveler, be he on snowshoes, skis, snowmobile, or foot, must be aware of the potential danger of snow slides anytime he is in hilly terrain. Avalanches have influenced man's thinking in the snow country since before Hannibal and his ambitious adventures through the Alps. Nature causes most slides but man has contributed his share, wittingly and unwittingly.

Strangely, when the Italian and Austrian armies faced each other in the embattled Austrian Alps during World War I, more deaths were caused by manmade avalanches as part of the battle strategy than by shells and bullets. More than 16,000 casualties were reported from deliberate slides in one four-day period. Man, through ignorance or calculated risk, still takes a grim toll of his own making on all continents where snow is piled up in sufficient quantities to slide when provoked.

There is no simple rule of thumb to gauge when and where a snow avalanche will let go, but there is a rule of thumb that says be ever conscious that the law of gravity is always in force. As Lowell Thomas says in one of the U.S. Forest Service's avalanche films, "give it a mountain to slide on and enough snow and you'll have an avalanche."

Statistics are now being kept of all reported snow avalanches in the United States and it is becoming increasingly clear that the small slide on the small hill is as much of a killer, trapping the unbeliever, as the big mountain slide. In the so-called gentle mountains of Vermont in the winter of 1969–70 snow slides covered major roads, routes 12 and 14 to name two. That cars were not caught in them was sheer luck — luck induced by the fact that the slides came during a severe storm during which travel was restricted. Two youngsters were caught in a snow slide while playing on an open hill just outside of Barre, Vermont, a few years ago and, if it hadn't been for one of their companions flagging down a rural mail carrier — who ran to the site with a shovel and dug them out — it would have been fatal. They could not have survived another hour. In another not so happy instance just a few years ago, two New York boys were killed by a very small avalanche that came down on them through some brush on a 35 degree slope of only 300 yards.

If it seems that we are putting the cart before the horse in discussing these isolated incidents, before detailing snow slides in general, we are doing so deliberately. We want to dispel the average winter traveler's notion that "it couldn't happen here," or that such things only happen in the Alps.

It isn't just skiers or boys playing who get caught; unwary snowshoe travelers too have become victims. One such tale is told by Dale Gallagher in *Snowy*

Avalanche country. In spite of its peaceful outlook, this terrain — with its steep slopes and deep snows — is high-risk territory for the mountaineering snowshoer. GENE PRATER PHOTO

Torrents, a handbook published by the U.S. Department of Agriculture in January, 1967. One day about 1:00 P.M., three men from an electric company near Ashton, Idaho, went by snowshoes to repair an electric line at a radio relay station 12 miles from the nearest highway. They started across a slope about a quarter mile below the relay staion when a 400-foot-wide avalanche released above them. One of the men saved himself by holding on to a tree, one man was completely engulfed by the snow, the third was injured by the crushing force of the snow but remained on the surface of the half-mile slide and was rescued, though later died of his injuries. It was 6:00 A.M. the following morning before a search party could reach the slide area, but by noon 70 people were engaged in the rescue effort. At 12:30 a snowshoe was found and a half-hour later the body of the missing man was located under five feet of snow. He was nearly three hundred feet from where the slide first caught him and forty feet in from the edge of the slide. The snow was piled over twenty feet deep at this point. There was a deep gash on his forehead and some snow had melted about his mouth indicating that the victim may have lived for a short time. If so, his fate was another sad result of the fact that rescue operations timely enough to recover buried victims are almost impossible in inaccessible areas.

This is only one more of many such avalanche disasters and is mentioned for the sole purpose of reminding the reader to take the possibility of avalanches seriously on all field trips.

Avalanche Causes

What conditions act to cause avalanches? In order of importance they are: snow conditions, shape of the slope, steepness of the slope, weather, growth or vegetation, and exposure (direction the slope faces).

SNOW CONDITIONS

New Snow. Enough loose new snow on a hard base may slide on slopes of 25 degrees. An accumulation of 12 inches is considered sufficient providing the old base is slippery enough (ie., a hard sun or rain crust).

If the snow were dug down to ground level a profile of the many layers of snow from past storms would be visible. It would show what happens to the snow in its transition from new snow to ice. At ground level may be found what is called depth hoar, small ice cups like hollow hail stones. This depth hoar is caused by moisture in the snow interacting with temperature changes from ground heat—alternately melting and freezing. Depth hoar sometimes builds up to many inches and provides a very unstable surface on which new snow can cling, however precariously. Whenever falling snow builds up on this surface at the rate of an inch an hour or more it is considered dangerous and may slide anytime it is disturbed.

Wet Snow. Wet snow slides can be especially devastating even though they slide more slowly and at a more predictable time. This is because they quickly solidify to a concrete texture when they stop. Wet snow slides are common in the springtime and occur in the same paths year after year. However, if the snow has built up and rain and warm winds combine, a wet snow slide can be expected on steep slopes at any time of the year, just as mud slides may be expected after extensive rains in certain areas on the California coast.

Snow Slabs.   Avalanches which are formed from snow which breaks off in large blocks and in clean fracture lines are called wind slab avalanches. They are so named not because wind triggers the slides but from the fact that the slabs are formed by wind action. These slabs are usually found on lee slopes and are formed either by blowing snow being dropped on a lee slope or by a warm wind blowing across the snow into a slope, in either case causing the snow to compact in such a way that it locks to itself but not to the snow layer beneath. Usually an air space forms between the slab layer and the under layers. This slab condition is easy to detect (if there is no new snow on top) because it has a dull chalky appearance and does not reflect light. It may be a few inches thick, or it may be many inches thick and may well support a man walking. The danger is not knowing what may trigger a fracture of this snow cover. It slides in blocks, quickly gathers momentum and most often carries any loose snow under it along too, at times down to ground level.

Snow Cornices.   Cornices are made in a similar fashion to slabs but are formed at the top of ridges by wind blowing the snow toward the edge of the ridge. This snow clings to itself and builds a false ridge which may extend a few feet out in space. It takes beautiful shapes and makes a lovely picture but it is treacherous and unstable, especially if you walk on it or are caught under it when it breaks off. And, if the conditions are ripe, when it falls it often starts the snow below to slide as well.

SLOPE STEEPNESS

Extreme steepness of slope is not always a principal factor in snow slides because anything steeper than 60 degrees avalanches almost continually, thereby keeping the snow from building up to dangerous depths. Furthermore, anything that steep should make even the most unwary look twice and not get caught. However, slopes anywhere from 25 to 75 degrees *are* susceptible to snow slides.

SLOPE SHAPE

An important thing to keep in mind is the shape of the slope. When a slope's profile shows its shape to be convex, the most tension on the snow cover would be at the top of the curve (although slides on these slopes have been known to break at the lower transition point). A concave slope would have the most pressure at the foot. On a uniform slope, the fracture line, or starting point, could be anywhere there is mass enough above waiting for the right trigger. And of course any slope may have any combination of these shapes.

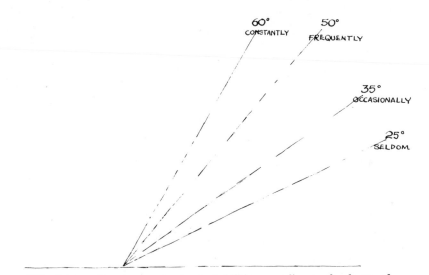

This diagram forecasts avalanche probabilities according to the degree of slope involved.

VEGETATION

The vegetation under the snow cover may be as influential in bonding the snow cover as any growth still appearing above the snow line. Long grassy slopes offer no inhibition to slides. Scrub growth, short grass, well-anchored rock, and very uneven ground offer good anchors until the snow depth covers it all and you have a new surface. Heavy timber usually is a deterrent to free-flowing snow slides, unless the snow gets a good start from high open slopes way above. Hummocks, gullies and ravines help break up an area and cause the snow to compact and anchor itself as it folds into the ground.

WEATHER

Weather conditions are a strong factor in avalanche making. Once avalanche conditions exist all that is needed is a trigger, and often that trigger is a weather change. A rapid rise in temperature after a heavy fall of wet snow on an old base could cause the melt to lubricate the old surface, making conditions ripe for a wet slide. A rapid fall in the temperature after a fall of new powder snow would prevent the snow from settling and bonding, making a slide most likely, providing all the other ingredients—mass, shape, steepness, and lack of barriers—are also present. Another factor to be considered under weather is the wind, which can aid in settling the snow or in helping to produce slab conditions.

Triggers

What is needed to release a slide? All that is needed is something to break the sometimes delicate bond or cohesion of the snow—perhaps the shock waves

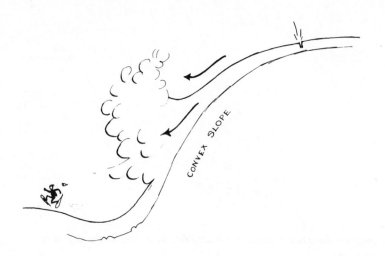

Slope shape plays an important role in the making of avalanches. This diagram shows a convex and a concave slope: both can be dangerous.

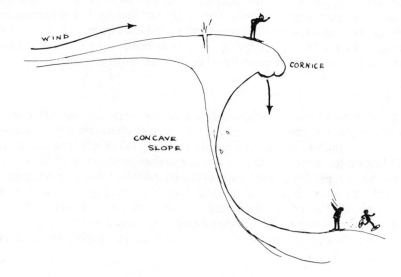

from some sound, an abrupt change in temperature, an overload of snow causing the force of gravity to win over cohesion, the shearing of the snow cover by a skier or snowshoer or some snow vehicle. Any of these things, under the right conditions, can trigger a slide.

SLAB SNOW SLIDE

It may only take a skier's or snowshoer's weight cutting the snow to cause a slab snow slide. The fracture line appears instantly and audibly (with a dull whumpf) as the air is compressed under the weight of the slab as it settles and breaks.

DRY SNOW SLIDE

A sound wave alone can trigger a dry snow slide. Even a loud shout has been known to start one. This type of slide starts at a point and rapidly fans out as it speeds down the slope often in excess of 100 miles an hour and with an accompanying snow dust cloud. The high speed causes air turbulence strong enough to pick up bulldozers, dump trucks and even houses, moving them or smashing them to pieces. Speeds have been clocked at over 200 miles per hour.

WET SNOW SLIDE

These slides are not necessarily triggered but occur when enough weight succumbs to the pull of gravity.

A snow cornice breaking off from above can trigger a slide, or ice hanging over a slope and falling on the snow beneath, with the added weight just enough to upset the balance. The sonic boom of an aircraft has been known to start a slide.

Happily, man's own devices can cause slides where and when wanted in order to make certain areas safe. Explosives in the form of artillery shells, compressed gas guns, or hand placed charges can be used to clear unsettled snow from threatening slopes. This is done by the daring but soundly trained Snow Rangers of the U.S. Forest Service.

Travel Precautions

There are certain precautions which should be taken when traveling in avalanche prone terrain. One should always survey the territory as one goes. Estimate slope steepness and check slope exposures. Determine prevailing wind directions and choose the windward slopes: they are safer. Look for signs of small slides, "sloughs," which indicate avalanche conditions are present. Do not travel in a narrow-bottomed valley with avalanche prone slopes above you. If crossing a suspected slide area, cross as high up on the slope as possible. Cross one at a time, staying behind natural barriers (that is, below them) so as not to be swept against one. The slides may flow around such obstacles. If in a group, someone should be appointed to watch the slope above while the rest are picking their way across.

When crossing the slope itself, everyone should loosen their gear and snowshoe bindings to enable them to throw everything off in a split second if necessary. A scarf should be worn around the face to cover the mouth and nose to prevent snow dust from getting in the airway in the event of a slide. Further, all should have colored avalanche cords trailing out behind them; the theory being that the cord would bounce along on the surface of any slide and, being light, would stay on top. The searchers would then hopefully spot the free end and find the victim at the other end. This cord is usually nylon, about thirty to fifty feet in length and ⅛ inch in diameter.

Helpful Hints

If you should be engulfed in sliding snow, there are some helpful movements worth trying. Use a swimming motion with the arms and hands kept up near the face and try to stay on your back. An abbeviated breast stroke is recommended, much as you would use for swimming from under water to the surface, except for the leg kicks. Keeping the hands near the face helps to create an air space and to avoid having the hands pinned down. (Many suffocation deaths in the snow are due to lack of air space and from the snow being crammed down the mouth and air passages.) Staying on your back facilitates your trying to dig yourself out.

Dig slowly if it is at all possible to move the snow. You can determine which way is up by the pull of gravity on something held up to dangle, such as a watch strap. Don't be surprised if this shows you to be upside down. Sound does travel in snow but do not shout or scream until you hear someone looking for you. Breathe as quietly as possible to save energy and air.

At the same time your companions should be probing for you with whatever instruments they can find (ie., ski poles, staffs, etc.). The search should start from the last spot at which you were observed and work down the fall line scuffing the snow and probing, looking for clothing or equipment and stopping to holler every few steps. This should be continued for an hour with careful watch for more slides being kept all the while. Outside help should not be sought for at least an hour if it would seriously cripple a speedy search of the area. After an hour, if party strength permits, two should be sent for help; no one should travel alone unless absolutely necessary. The remaining party members should recheck the pile-up area and any areas where the snow may have been diverted around an obstacle.

When you (or anyone) are found buried, the rescuers should dig carefully with their hands when near the body. Standard first aid procedure upon recovery is self-evident, with special attention to the need for artificial respiration and the rewarming of the whole body. Exposure to cold and the subsequent lowered body temperature is inevitable.

The Odds

The grim statistics show that chances for survival for anyone buried under more than two feet of snow for more than an hour are only about thirty percent; for anyone buried in less than two feet there is about a fifty percent chance of successful rescue, if it is accomplished within half an hour. For those who like long odds, survival has been recorded up to seventy-two hours. In one extremely rare case in Norway, a successful rescue was recorded after the victim was buried for one week in a springtime wet snow slide. All these long-term burial survivals were by victims who were conscious and who did not have ice masks form to cut off their air (ice masks form around the mouth from exhaled breath from the mouth or nose which condenses and freezes when the victim is unconscious). And, in the Norwegian case, brush had provided air spaces and an airway through the snow above.

It is not the intent of this section to offer an avalanche course or furnish all the answers. However, it is its intent to create enough interest to lead the reader to seek out and attend a course or orientation lecture on avalanches, such as usually offered by local National Ski Patrol avalanche instructors or by Forest Service personnel. Write them or check with your local club, but do keep yourself posted, and do obey all avalanche warning signs posted in mountain terrain.

WINTER RESCUE

Each year there are many emergencies requiring search and recovery operations in all types of snowy terrain — mountainous, rolling, wooded and open. Much attention has already been directed to the forming of trained and equipped rescue units to work over the entire snow-belted North American continent. This has paid off but the demand still exceeds the supply. As more and more people hit the snow country on skis, snowshoes and snow machines, more and more emergencies are inevitable — to say nothing of the incidents involving downed airplanes, lost hunters, snowbound travelers, and stranded mountain climbers.

Emergency recoveries in snow country have been aided greatly by dependable over-snow machines. Sometimes, however, the machines fail or get bogged down or the operator gets hurt and any would-be rescuers are back on their own two feet again. As snow over a foot deep is too tiring to walk through, snowshoes are still the best answer.

Rescues come under several different headings:

A. Unplanned — usually on a small scale, perhaps from a sudden call from friends.
B. Self Rescue — an individual or his party is stranded.
C. Pre-planned — an organized effort by a trained rescue unit (National Ski Patrol, Air Search and Rescue team, Civil Air Patrol, etc.).

Unplanned Rescues

These are regretfully more common than realized. Such a rescue might happen like this. A friend's wife calls about suppertime to say that her husband hasn't returned from his snowshoe trip though he'd said he'd be back several hours before dark. And off you go. What you need is a friend or two, equipment for the weather, headlamp or flashlight, first aid kit, emergency repair kit or, better yet, a spare pair of snowshoes and a map of your friend's favorite tripping area or someone who knows the area well. A voice gun might be helpful if you can get it in a hurry. Chances are that Jack has broken a snowshoe and is floundering along, so hopefully it will just be a matter of trying to pick up his tracks. Take along some hot tea or bouillon. Flavor the tea with a generous spoonful of honey for quick energy. Your friend may be tired and this form of pickup is far better than the variety loved by many but better saved for when the rescued and rescuers are safely back indoors.

Self-Rescue

The chief essential in this situation is prior training and use of the skills involved in survival living. This means always carrying all necessary items for emergency repairs to equipment or self, along with a reserve food pack and extra garment for the nighttime chill. Fire-making tools would prove handy for making signal fires should you be disabled or just for morale boosting. Your map and compass would be an integral part of any self-rescue, though it's worth saying that sometimes in these situations one is not lost — just confused. In this case, the best thing to do is just stay put for the night.

If the time comes when there is the slightest doubt about being lost or having to stay out all night on an unplanned bivouac, make the decision to stop before fatigue sets in. Fatigue is insidious; most people will deny its existence. But the disciplined outdoor traveler will recognize when he is becoming overtired and will take immediate steps to recover. He knows that his best asset is a "thinking brain;" so he stops to rest, consumes some food to replenish his body fuel (body heat), and makes sure his environment is protected from wind and wetness.

Once a decision has been made to go no further there are certain basic steps to be taken. (1) Try to assess the situation calmly. (2) To the best of your collective knowledge, decide where you are. (3) Figure the time it took you to get where you are from the last known source of help and/or shelter, realizing that it would take that much time or longer to get back, depending on the terrain, visibility, worsening snow conditions or breakdown of equipment necessary for movement. (4) Estimate your remaining daylight hours. (5) Make an inventory and pool all available resources, including food and water, equipment in your pockets, any extra clothing, etc.

Then under the assumption that this is strictly an emergency bivouac in *wooded* terrain and that you have neither sleeping bags, ground cloths or tents, first pick a spot to make camp by seeking natural windbreaks, such as under trees, against large boulders, or in burrows under blow-downs. Once the spot is picked, pack down the snow and gather wood for a fire. Remember that you are now concerned with survival, not ecology, so gather whatever insulation material you can find: boughs, branches, grass or bullrushes found by digging under the snow—whatever is dry. Then make a place to sit down rather than to lie down. The seat should be as low as needed to get out of the wind. Pad the seat with whatever is available so you will not melt the snow under it or get wet in any way. Put some insulation material down underfoot to help keep everyone's feet out of the snow. Build your fire only after each member has a place and you have gathered enough wood and that much more again.

It is essential to conserve energy; so all this preparation should be at a slow pace. This will help keep everyone calm and prevent working up a sweat. Stay together, assign tasks, and rotate them. If you have not eaten, once your protective shelter and fireplace are prepared and the wood gathered, fix a meal, but remember to keep a reserve of food according to your estimate of how long it may be before you get back to shelter. You need the food for energy and heat. Ration it fairly and according to needs. If there are exhausted members, they should be fed first, kept warm, and made to conserve their strength. Do not work until exhausted and, at all costs, keep dry (wet clothes conduct body heat away faster than dry ones).

Once you have eaten, sit close together to share body heat. Rotate the chores and the fire watch, letting the others doze off. In addition to feeding the fire, the fire watch should keep tabs to be sure that any clothes drying or feet being warmed are not too close to the fire. The fire watcher should also have a good fan to stir up a draft whenever the fire gets low.

Morning will come after what seems a very long night, but with it will come fresh hope and new ideas of what to do (i.e., stay put and wait for help or try to work your way back). If the decision is to leave, consider how you might safely lighten your pack. Decide what is absolutely necessary for travel and safety, leaving the rest in a well-marked spot. A lighter load can make a big difference on the return trip.

If the decision is to stay, or the group is in trouble, signal fires can and should be prepared. The decision as to when to light them should be based on the availability of more fuel, the time that people may be searching, the presence of aircraft, etc. Green wood and boughs will make smoke dense enough to be seen if the wind isn't blowing too hard. The fire should be laid in as open a spot as possible. The use of a signal mirror should be practiced so that it can be quickly focused when the occasion arises.

If caught in the open without cover or shelter of any kind, whether above timberline or not, the necessary self-rescue procedures will, of course, have to vary. Shelter from the wind is the first priority. Dig down to construct a snow slit trench, or if you can not dig down, build up. A snow wall built in the right wind direction will prove itself.

All the steps for emergency bivouac in timber apply here with the obvious exceptions of doing without a wood fire and without the insulation from gathered wood materials. Care must be exercised to protect against getting clothing wet when digging in the snow and handling snow blocks for wall building. Rotation of jobs should include checking each other for cold symptoms, injuries and degree of consciousness. The sit instead of lie down idea may have to be discarded and huddling together for warmth practiced in earnest. Every bit of insulation material must be utilized. If there is enough snow to construct a shelf to sleep on, it is worth the effort. Roofing the shelter may be possible with what is at hand. The snowshoes themselves can be used to provide a barrier between the snow and the user when lying down, or to provide roof support upon which snow can be piled to help trap escaping body heat in the shelter. Any external source of heat, even the heat of a candle, can be significant.

Pre-planned Rescues

In a situation involving a pre-planned group rescue, some official body of authority would assume the overall resonsibility—whether it be the police, fish and game department, U.S. Forest Service, or whatever. Members of these groups are well trained in this work and would of course do the planning and directing. However, they often call on volunteers to help and it is our hope that the following might prove helpful to any seasoned snowshoer who might want to join such a rescue operation.

Once an emergency has been declared, certain information is essential before a reasonable plan of action can be formed. What happened? Where? When? Who is involved? What is the probable cause? Every effort must be made to get the answers to as many of these questions as possible before the rescue plan is drawn up.

The director of the operation must choose his field leaders and brief them as thoroughly as possible. Speed is important but not always the paramount consideration. This briefing would include the following: 1) a statement of the operation's objective in as much detail as possible; 2) an estimation of the situation, including time, weather, terrain, support groups, chances of success, degree of urgency, etc.; 3) an outline of the plan, giving group assignments, areas of responsibility, etc. At the same time the administrative details concerning such things as equipment, food and personnel would be covered, communications arrangements outlined and safety precautions gone over.

HEADQUARTERS

A headquarters must be established—generally at the end of a road, the last spot wheeled vehicles can reach. This can be a house, school, camp, tent, bus, etc., but hopefully something heated with enough room for the workers, press, and next of kin. It should also include a supply depot for all the necessary equipment and, if at all possible, medical help should be available. Sometimes, in an area that might attract sightseers, even restraining lines must be provided.

A communications center should be established where messages can be logged in and out and a chronological account kept. A situation map should be adjacent to the log to mark the field parties' progress, pinpoint new areas and block out those already screened.

A word might be said here about the necessity for consideration of the next of kin concerned in these rescue operations which can sometimes become tragedies. Cruel or careless talk or expressions of doubts as to the efficiency of the operation must not be allowed to reach them. It only adds to the worry and heartbreak.

GETTING READY

Before rescuers can be dispatched, they must be equipped. Each rescuer should have his own emergency kit, including — as we have said before — snowshoe repair items, spare thongs, jackknife, light, extra clothing, food, and a compass. He should also have a map premarked with known landmarks and zones of responsibility and signaling devices as planned. Group equipment should include the rescue sleds or ahkios with hauling harness, axes, saws, machetes, first aid equipment, notebooks and pencils, and perhaps lightweight stokes litters with material to convert them to sleds. Lightweight but strong shovels are a must, as are ropes for steep terrain and ice areas and perhaps for crossing doubtful frozen ponds. Snow vehicles, when available, should also be included, along with portable stoves for cooking and heat, with fuel for same.

TRAIL BREAKING

The method of operation would depend upon the leader's instructions, but prior practice in hauling sleds, breaking trail, and controlling sleds on difficult terrain would be invaluable and eliminate any surprise as to how hard the going can be in these situations.

Trail breaking and sled or toboggan handling in rescue work can be eased with thoughtful planning and careful attention to terrain and route selection. Consider the following: the rate of travel for a snowshoe column in unbroken snow cross country in variable terrain is about 1 to 1-½ miles per hour; on a broken-out trail, 2 to 2-½ miles per hour. Minimum safe thickness for ice crossing (in single file) on foot is 4 inches, perhaps 1-½ to 2 inches when on skis or snowshoes. Wet snow or water under the snow will cause difficulties as it tends to freeze to the webbing, adding considerable weight and loss of stability; in these cases the trail should be broken out and reinforced with brush and boughs.

When the trail is to be used by sleds (man hauled), it must be broken out even if speed is essential. The sleds will ride higher, haul easier and flotation is better. To break trail for sleds at least three people should do the job. The leader (or point) trying to hit the center line of the planned route and the two follow-up trailbreakers covering one of the leader's tracks with his inside foot and making a new track with his outside foot. This will result in a track at least four shoes wide. This is usually wide enough for a sled team hauling in single file. If possible, pick the snowshoe to fit the terrain and snow cover. Swap leads constantly. Set a time limit, no exhausted heroes needed.

SLED HANDLING

Pick routes that for the most part lead straight up and down the steep sections. This will avoid sideslipping and off-the-track relay lines. On very steep sections ropes can be utilized to belay around trees in the line and allow for rests while holding the sled in place. The sleds should be hauled by men in file, using harnesses made (or improvised) to allow the pull to be straight back from each hauler without cutting off his wind or pulling on his stomach. The hands must be left free to dig in with the poles to add traction when necessary. The belay technique can be utilized to control the descent of the sled on steep pitches. Sometimes two "tail gunners" can be used to advantage when going downhill, with only one in front to keep the sled in line. On a traverse it may be necessary for men to be placed uphill and to the sides to control sideslipping with additional ropes. No one should try to haul a sled for any but short distances with just a rope held in the hands. Tying a loop in the rope big enough to allow a bight to go over the shoulder would be an improvement on the hand-held technique. The loop over the shoulder would allow the hands and arms to be free to use the ski poles as mentioned. This technique can also be used effectively with more than one man. Three can haul a 200 lb. load without too much trouble under favorable terrain and trail conditions. Hauling a sled with a casualty on it naturally requires considerably more care and attention. When establishing a route to the casualty, thought should be given to utilizing the same trail on the way out. Surveyors' yellow plastic marking tape can be used to indicate rescue routes. Yellow is best as it is unmistakable to colorblind people and is fast becoming accepted as the best for emergency use. When the rescue route is no longer needed, the tape should be removed to avoid confusion.

Some traverses may require that the trail be made level in order not to aggravate an injury by tipping the sled too sharply. On a steep icy trail a fixed rope may prove useful, and the time spent establishing it well worth the while. This is, of course, if trained mountaineers are available. It involves a rope handrail anchored to trees or rocks, keeping the rope taut and about waist high.

"Belaying" a loaded ahkio during a steep decline.

It can be used to tie in to so rest halts can be made on these steep slopes without fear of losing the sled. The sled itself can be tied in to the rope. Prusik slings will ensure that the sled will not get away if the load has to be belayed up or down, snaplinks or carabiners are also useful. Installations of this type are a great help for operations in the dark, on slippery terrain, and for weary climbers carrying heavy loads.

When hauling a casualty, rescuers should keep their voices down when discussing terrain and other difficulties. Be sure the casualty's hands are inside. Someone near the head should be assigned to keep an eye on the victim, to converse if necessary and to cheer up as required. The victim's face should be watched for any change in condition and any displaced snow kept off his face and body to eliminate as much chilling and wetting as possible.

In the cold, frequent 30-second to 2-minute rest breaks for breathing "blows" are better than infrequent but longer ones. Change crews on schedule and be sure to equalize the work load.

The Wrap Up

The rescue effort must come to an end at some point, hopefully with success. But successful or not, there is always the tiresome job of cleaning up all the details. A report must be written, agencies notified, equipment returned, expenses taken care of, and workers checked-off and thanked — all necessary parts of this important and demanding work.

7 | A WINTER CAMP

We have had so many good times using snowshoes to get to a winter campsite that we thought we would share a few of the techniques that have been especially useful and some reminders of what to avoid. For, to paraphrase Nessmuk, that famous outdoorsman, we believe that the purpose of camping is not to "rough it" but to "smooth it." For a comprehensive and very readable look at the winter camping scene we recommend *Movin' On* by Harry Roberts.

The Toboggan Camp

Our experience leads us to suggest the idea of a toboggan camp as a means of combining transportation with overnight sleeping quarters. It's well known, of course, that a toboggan is an excellent means of sliding a considerable load over the snow with minimal effort wherever the terrain is not too steep. What we do is lay out our sleeping bag over the toboggan mattress; distribute various articles of our camping gear over the sleeping bag so that the heavy items are loaded to the rear; envelop the whole with a light tarpaulin to keep the snow off, and we're ready to go with our snowshoes over the wintry trails. When time comes to turn in for the night, we just sack out right there on the toboggan, making sure beforehand that it is perfectly level and secure. Who wants to go sliding downhill and crash into a tree right in the middle of a pleasant dream? If snow is falling during the night, we use the tarpaulin as a snow shield; otherwise no covering is necessary, and we can gaze at the stars far out there in the void, perfectly secure in the comfortable confines of the toboggan camp. Next morning there is no sleeping bag to stuff or lots of gear to arrange in the pack sack; we just load up the toboggan and are off again with a minimum of fuss.

Now just a few words about the toboggan. Most modern ones have parallel sides. It is really worthwhile to shave down the sides a bit to give a tapering effect so that the tail is narrower than the nose. It slides more easily that way. Indians most always made their toboggans with tapering sides. Listen to the voice of experience!

Now about hauling the toboggan. Two ways we have found to be quite good. Considering that we might want a day pack for items to be quickly accessible without the inconvenience of unlashing the toboggan cover, we use the day pack as a hauling harness. It works best if the pack is of the rucksack type with a belly strap. We bring a light cord from the top of the pack out to the rear and hook it to the toboggan with that ingenious hitch called the Arctic Toggle. This was invented by the Inuit as a means of quickly hitching up their dog teams without having to tie knots. A toggle is a transverse pin placed through the eye of a rope and it is simplicity itself to hitch the toggle of the day pack to the toboggan toggle. Just as easy to unhitch, once the tension is off. An even lighter harness is a loop of 2″ webbing strap just long enough to go under the armpits and around the back of the neck with a single hauling cord back to the toboggan tied into the loop of webbing. Snowshoes are ideal for sled hauling. We especially like to use the modern types with built-in traction aids and sturdy bindings mounted on a pivot pin. Ski poles or the winter staff help to give that extra assist whenever needed.

Simplify!

We have always approved of Henry Thoreau's famous statement, "Simplify, Simplify!", and we see a classic example of this in the form of a winter camp which is made by just using snow and snowshoes. This had been developed long ago by the Athabaskan Indians as a hunting shelter. They called it the quin-zhee. The way they built and used it on their hunting journeys is vividly described by William O. Pruitt in his excellent book, *Animals of the North* (Harper & Row, 1967).

If you are not a claustrophobe, you will find the quin-zhee very comfortable indeed, for, as experimenters have found, with outside temperatures at $-60°$ F, the inside will be at or just above the freezing point because of the insulating qualities of the snow and the intrinsic warmth streaming up from the earth below.

A quin-zhee for five requires a mound of snow ten feet in diameter at the base by five feet high. Quin-zhees differ from the igloos, or snowhouses of the Inuit, in that the quin-zhee is made of loose snow while the igloo is made from blocks cut from the highly wind-compacted tundra snow. In building a quin-zhee, snowshoes themselves or the shovel end of the Winter Staff can be used to heap loose snow into that required mound shape. After cold, loose snow is tossed and mounded, it sets up almost like concrete in about two hours time so that it is possible to excavate a sleeping chamber into the mound without any fear of it collapsing. Plan to have base thickness of the walls about 18″ and the top not more than 8″. If unsure about how the excavations are proceeding, punch a stick through the sides from time to time and take some measurements. In very cold regions where the ground surface is quite dry, as in the boreal forest, sweep the floor of the quin-zhee free of snow and place caribou skins or Ensolite pads directly on the ground surface. Where the ground surface might be damp, as in more temperate regions, leave a well-packed snow surface as the floor of the quin-zhee as this will be warmer than a soggy dirt floor. Plenty of insulation between the body and surface below is a key factor in comfortable winter camping.

Classical quin-zhees have always been meant for sleeping only — never for any fires inside; therefore, it was never necessary to allow for vent holes, and the entryway was always stuffed up tight after everyone was inside to preserve all possible heat. Enough air passes through this type of snow to allow for oxygen consumption of sleeping occupants of a quin-zhee.

Tents

When tents are considered for winter overnights, they should have frost liners, waterproof sewed-in floors, air vents, entrances that can be gathered and closed tight, poles that will not freeze together, and a protected vestibule or equivalent space for cooking. More headroom in the tent makes for easier inside changing but must be compared against increased weight. Recreational equipment catalogues and excellent outdoor magazines provide up-to-date sources for many types of tents to suit a variety of conditions, but not necessarily checking accounts. This is where the quin-zhee comes on strong at the winter camp.

Campfires and Stoves

Blazing fires make the winter camp a place of real comfort and appeal. Around the campfire we think atavistic thoughts about mastodons and wolves, and feel secure in the blazing light; and comfortable, may we add, in the nice warmth. A good campfire is a *sine qua non*, although we know that these days there are many places where a fire would be out of the question because of land use requirements. Sometimes, though, with a bit of ingenuity, it is quite possible to set up the winter camp close by an area that has recently been cut over and where there is a huge abundance of waste wood. Always get permission from landowners before camping, whether you intend to build fires or not. Good relations established in this way can yield benefits in the form of more and better campsites in years to come.

Of course, campfires bring up the subject of smoke in the eyes and the aggravation of having it seemingly follow everyone everywhere. We don't pretend to have the magic solution to this nuisance, but we have found from long experience that if it is possible to locate the campsite in a shallow ravine with the fire on the downside of the camp, natural air drainage patterns will keep most of the smoke out of the camp.

Where campfires are out of the question then stoves make a good alternative. Those using gasoline as a fuel are probably the best to use in cold weather, while a fuel like butane is not so good because it won't vaporize at low temperatures. The possibility of carbon monoxide poisoning is *always* present whenever any types of fuel are burned in an enclosed space. Never forget this, for there is no reason to turn a pleasant winter camping trip into a deadly disaster. Carbon monoxide poisoning is an insidious robber of good sense, even of the most sophisticated winter travellers. Admiral Byrd at Little America almost succumbed to carbon monoxide poisoning. Take heed and never get into that same trap.

Rules of the North

It is especially convenient if that same little valley selected for the campsite as a reason to keep smoke out of the eyes, also has a stream flowing through it. Why bother to melt snow when you could use the winter staff to cut through a little ice to get at the fresh water flowing below? Another excellent location for the winter camp is adjacent to a pond or small lake for another unlimited supply of water. After a hole has been cut through the ice, fill it in with loose, fluffy snow to prevent a hard freeze again. Mark this location with a stick or the universal symbol of the spruce bough so to be able to find it again and to keep anyone from falling into the hole. This is a rule of the North.

Another rule of the North which, unfortunately, is too often overlooked is to boil or properly treat all water from whatever source it may come. Wilderness water cannot be guaranteed safe even though there are no obvious sources of contamination. A small organism called *Giardia lamblia* is almost universally found in northern waters. This microscopic creature can cause a most uncomfortable and persistent form of diarrhea compared to which "Montezuma's Revenge" is mild indeed.

While the tolerance for error is much smaller at a winter camp than for a comparable summer camp, we feel that the rewards and satisfactions that come from establishing a pleasant and comfortable winter camp are great indeed. And just think; there is no need at all for bug dope!

FUN AND GAMES
ON SNOWSHOES

Of course an organized snowshoe race takes a lot of dedicated interest, not only by the racers, but by many others who serve faithfully on the sidelines or in the background; such people as judges, timers, track stompers, etc. For something a bit less demanding and open to all here are some ideas for games that can be played on snowshoes:

Compass Game

For the compass game, nine players and a referee tramp out something rather resembling a wheel in the snow, the rim being about three snowshoes wide and the center area about ten yards across. Mark out a bulge or niche in the snow where North, South, West and East would be on the wheel. Then add bulges for the Northeast, Southeast, Southwest and Northwest. Connect them all to the center, or hub, like the spokes of a wheel. Station players at all the designated compass points and select one to be "it" or the "needle" in the center. Each person has to remember what compass point he is and what point the other players represent. The referee will call out two different points of the compass and the two players representing these points will try to exchange places. At the same time the player in the middle tries to beat one of them to the vacated compass point. If "it" or the "needle" wins, the displaced player moves to the middle. The fun begins when, after a few shifts of position, the players forget their new positions and "it" starts to beat them to the spots. Any shortcuts between compass points is permissable, both for the needle and the points themselves. (If azimuths were used the approximate numbers called would be 360 and 180, 90 and 270, 45, and 135, or any combination thereof. This would really sharpen wits!)

In this game, everyone sharpens their sense of direction and has a good time as well. It can be an effective teaching device for the trip-minded youngster. Various changeoffs can be instituted such as having the players change place with the referee or having extra players fill in and change the circle completely to further confuse matters.

If the snow is over six inches deep, the entire circle may be tramped down to facilitate changing positions. However, the fun will be even greater and the laughs louder if everyone is just left to flounder as they try to run through the deep snow.

Fox and Geese

Fox and geese can be played on the same circle as the compass game but preferably before, as once this lively game starts the wheel soon becomes unrecognizable due to the many criss-crossing tracks. In fox and geese, the fox stays in the middle while the geese run around the outside rim and dare him to catch them. He, the fox, must catch them between spokes on the rim, so there can't be too many spokes and enough distance between them to give the fox a chance.

Dodge Ball

Dodge ball on snowshoes can be fun when played with a soft volleyball on a level area about the size of a basketball court. Establish the base lines and boundaries, mark the middle line, and choose sides. Someone throws in the ball, and then it's dodge and run for your life as each side tries to pick up the ball and then throw it to hit a man on the other side. If a player is hit, he drops out until the last survivor's team is declared the winner, or a time limit is set and the winner is determined by the number of players left on each side. No one is allowed to go outside the boundary line without being declared out. Only three steps can be taken before throwing the ball at another player. The ball may be passed behind the center line to players on the same side, and then thrown at an opposing player, but only twice before it must be thrown across the line, as in volleyball.

A Rough One

A form of field hockey can be played on snowshoes if a colored ball is used and the playing surface is well tramped. The ball should be smaller than a volleyball but larger than a lacrosse ball—about the size of a softball would be ideal. In fact, color a softball and try it. Helmets may be desirable if the play becomes too fierce. Spills will be the order of the day so lethal stick swinging near an opponent who is down should be curtailed.

Potatoes, Anyone?

For another kind of fun on snowshoes why not stage an old-fashioned potato race? For this event a basket is set in the center of a level snow-covered field or on the surface of a frozen lake. Potatoes, or similar objects, are then laid out at equal intervals in straight lines extending away from the basket in the same way that the spokes radiate outwards from the hub of a wheel. Each snowshoe-shod contestant is assigned to a line of potatoes and stands with the tail of his snowshoes to the basket just sufficiently distant from the basket so as not to interfere with his competitors and yet close enough so no one has an advantage at the start. At the word "Go," all run out to the first potato in their lines, pick it up and return to drop it in the basket. The process is continued until the winner

Bridging the generation gap with a rousing game of baseball on snowshoes. ALASKA TRAVEL BUREAU

has gotten all of the potatoes from his line into the basket before anyone else. It soon becomes obvious that this game requires great skill in manipulating snowshoes in addition to considerable running ability.

A Hard One

Or, try the ring race. Here the emphasis is laid on skill in getting into and out of snowshoe harnesses, as well as running on snowshoes and manipulating a ski pole. For this race, the contestants line up about ten yards behind their snowshoes which are laid out in pairs in a straight line pointing down the course. Each racer carries a single ski pole and, at the starting signal, must run forward, fasten on his snowshoes, and then run ahead along the course. Midway down the course, along each racer's track, a ring with an interior diameter of two inches is laid in the snow. Each contestant must pick up the ring on the tip of the ski pole, holding the pole in one hand at the upper end only, and then continue along the course to the end where a pin is set vertically in the snow. This pin should have a diameter only slightly less than the inside of the ring. On arriving at the pin, the racer must deposit the ring over the pin still holding the pole in one hand at the upper end only. After the ring is on the pin, the contestants run back to where they put on their snowshoes, then take them off and run back to the starting line. In such an event, the snowshoe bindings should be of similar style so that one racer does not have an advantage over another.

The Mad Trapper Event

This is staged at Whitehorse in Canada's Yukon Territory during February as one of the features of the Yukon Sourdough Rendezvous. The event is a test of survival skills where contestants race the clock by dashing into the bush; get a fire started; tea boiling; bannock baking, and a trap set — all on snowshoes of course!

These are only a few examples of games to play on snowshoes. No doubt you and your fellow snowshoers can think of many others to try — moments of sheer fun to add to all the other joys of snowshoeing.

SNOWSHOE RUNNING AND RACING

The United States Snowshoe Association (USSSA) has recently been promoting the idea of running or jogging on snowshoes. It's not really much of a job to break out a nice snow path in a series of loops, figure eights, or whatever pattern strikes the fancy. Choose the places for making snow paths where they will be convenient to run on as often as possible. As the paths are used frequently, they become compacted and have a nice, resilient feel underfoot (i.e., snowshoe). So much better than running on hard pavement; moreover, the hard pavements of the winter highways are usually heaped on either side with snow banks, making them very dangerous places for any type of foot traffic whether they be runners or walkers. We have tried snowshoe jogging on the local golf course and find the terrain ideally suited for this type of exercise. Also there is the convenient parking area to leave the cars.

Experienced runners find that the transition to snowshoes is very easy, and after they have tried it a few times, they become missionaries for the cause. Regular running clothes, and especially the light running shoes, fit well with snowshoes.

RUNNING EQUIPMENT

Snowshoes for running should be light, narrow, and well balanced. Some manufacturers make a special type of snowshoe for racing, and these are also very good for jogging (see list at the back of the book). But it is not really necessary to go out and buy a special pair for jogging, as practically any type will do just so they are not really heavy and cumbersome. Neoprene lacings and bindings have been widely accepted, but a word of caution is in order. There are varying grades and qualities of Neoprene, and some cheaper types have been appearing that are not proving durable under hard use in races over packed trails.

Bindings should be lightweight and easy to get in and out of. We like the sandal and thong binding described on p. 35. Simply cross the thongs behind the heels and tie the ends off right in front of the ankles. To make this secure we always tie it off with Linna's Knot. This useful variation on the standard

The joy of snowshoe jogging. NORWICH UNIVERSITY PHOTO SERVICE

Well-known Adirondack snowshoe maker, Carl E. Heilman II, prepares for a run on his special light racing Catpaw *snowshoes.* HEILMAN PHOTO

shoelace bow keeps it from coming untied under stress. To make Linna's Knot just pass the second bow back through the loop and tighten it up.

Another good snowshoe combination for running and racing is the *Sherpa Snow-Claw*; either the Featherweight, Lightfoot, or a special racing shoe called the Ultra-Light. The *Snow-Claw*, which is an integral part of the binding, would be a great help in getting off to a quick start (some race officials might even see this as giving too much of an advantage if not all were equipped with the same snowshoes).

Conditioning

Snowshoe runners who were also foot runners during the warm months don't have to think too much about being in condition for their exercise because they are already pretty fit. But for those who might like to take up snowshoe running for the first time, may we recommend that they take things quite easy at first and gradually build up a regimen of conditioning. One way of doing this during snowless times would be to wear extra heavy boots while out for a walk as this will strengthen muscles which will be carrying the snowshoe weight during the snow months. Persons going in for serious snowshoe racing need to adhere to a consistent type of training. Champion Joyce Haugen stresses the fact that dedicated training pays off. She should know!

Until quite recently, snowshoe racing was fairly limited to Canada's Province of Quebec and to a few communities in the northeastern United States. Snowshoe racing still continues to be popular there, but a surge of interest has swept over the northern tier of the United States. The Arctic Winter Games also attest to the fact that snowshoe racing has become firmly established in the far north.

Organizations

A variety of events are in store for the prospective snowshoe racer, ranging from short sprints to marathons and even snowshoe biathlons; all run on snowshoes from beginning to end. North American snowshoe racing enthusiasts will find that certain organizations set rules and regulations for the events. The Canadian Snowshoers' Union and the American Snowshoers' Union act together through an international committee. It sanctions the races referred to earlier, largely concentrated in the Province of Quebec and in certain communities of northeastern United States where there is a large French-speaking population. Persons wishing to know more about races sponsored by the clubs which belong to these Unions could contact Madame Magella Aidans who is the secretary-treasurer of the International Snowshoers' Committee. Her address is 2541 Jeanne D'Arc, Montreal, P.Q., Canada, H1W 3W1, phone (514) 259-1183.

Another organization that is especially interested in competitive snowshoe events is the United States Snowshoe Association (USSSA). Since its beginning in 1977 the USSSA has been on the move. Through the efforts of the organization and its friends, Corinth, New York, has been proclaimed the Snowshoe Capital of America, and a number of snowshoe races have been held

Racing or jogging can still be fun. Author Bill Osgood, Biology Professor Dr. Michael Sinclair and his wife Mary keep in shape for summer marathoning by snowshoe jogging. NORWICH UNIVERSITY PHOTO SERVICE

Stretching out. NORWICH UNIVERSITY PHOTO SERVICE

Only a few more steps to go. No. 83 approaches the finish line at the World Championship Centennial Snowshoe Meet held in Ottawa. CANADIAN TRAVEL BUREAU

in Corinth or in neighboring areas. Headquarters of the USSSA are P.O. Box 170, R.D. 1, Corinth, New York, 12822.

For information about competing in the Arctic Winter Games, write to Ted Richard, Director of the Board, Arctic Winter Games, Searle, Barrister & Solicitors, Yellowknife, NWT, Canada. This central office manages the administration of the games wherever they may be held. In 1980 they were held in Whitehorse, Yukon Territory, Canada.

These several organizations do not at this time share common rules and regulations for snowshoe racing, but there is an effort in this direction, primarily to lay some groundwork for a more widely established network of snowshoeing competitions throughout the cold regions of the world where snowshoeing might be enjoyed as much as it is here in North America.

Racing snowshoes do not as yet have common standards. Rules of the Canadian Snowshoers' Union stipulate that for the shorter events the snowshoes for both men and women be no smaller than nine by thirty-two inches. For the long distance events called marches the men's snowshoes must be no smaller than ten by forty inches and the women's no smaller than nine by thirty-three inches. The use of spikes as traction aids is prohibited. The United States Snowshoe Association rules that snowshoes used in its sanctioned events be no smaller than eight by twenty-five inches, but there is no restriction against traction aids. Sometimes special requirements may be set for certain races. For example, the Yukon Jack 83-mile marathon race specifies that all snowshoes used in the race must measure ten by twenty-eight inches or larger, and a pair of snowshoes with bindings must weigh at least three pounds ten ounces.

Events

Competitive snowshoe events are now almost universally stated in metric mesurements just as they are for track and field events. These include 100, 200, 400 and 800 meter sprints for both men and women, plus a special 50 meter sprint for women. For longer distances there is the 1,500 meter event, the metric mile, and the popular 1,500 meter relay for both men and women.

It is interesting to match the times posted by the winners in international snowshoe races against interscholastic foot race times that have been converted to meters.

Events	Track Times	Snowshoe Times
100 meters	11.95 seconds	16.5 seconds
200 meters	23.12 seconds	38.2 seconds
400 meters	51.52 seconds	1 minute 33.6 seconds
800 meters	1 minute 59.62 seconds	3 minutes 17.6 seconds
1500 meters	(no time)	6 minutes 23.8 seconds

These snowshoe racers show excellent form and really cover ground at the Pas-Trappers Festival. MANITOBA ARCHIVES

Taking the high hurdles before a large crowd at the North American Championship Sled Dog Race meet in Fairbanks. ALASKA TRAVEL BUREAU

In addition to the standard racing events, the United States Snowshoe Association has introduced the idea of a snowshoe slalom where the competitors are required to run downhill through a series of gates marked by flags. Ski poles are recommended and encouraged for the racers to use to help them get through the gates marked by flags which may not be touched or knocked down. The Association has also developed an innovative muzzle-loaded firearm snowshoe biathlon event where contestants fire at six targets positioned at equal distances 45 meters off the 16 kilometer course.

Another version of the snowshoe biathlon was initiated during the Winter Games on Mill Hill in Northfield, Vermont, in February, 1980. It was sponsored by the New England Chapter of the Tenth Mountain Division Association. This version uses shotguns at two shooting positions. Snowshoe gunners fire at moving targets in the form of clay pigeons, taking three shots at pigeons coming from the left and three shots from the right. The running part of the event comes between the two firing positions.

Snowshoe marathon races are also becoming quite popular. Wisconsin, for example, has two. One at Lyman Lake and the 83-mile event between Lake Superior and Rice Lake which takes three days to complete and has as one of its competitors a long distance champion snowshoer who also happens to be the mother of seven and grandmother of nine (at last count!). These two racing events offer cash prizes to the victors.

With the current interest growing in snowshoe racing, we would like to suggest that snowshoe orienteering be added to the list. Orienteering itself evolved in Scandinavia during the nineteenth century as a winter sport where skiers used map and compass to navigate through unfamiliar terrain. Later on, foot orienteering became even more popular. Both foot and ski orienteering (sometimes called Ski-O) have emigrated to North America in recent years with a small but devoted following to what has been called the "thinking person's sport." Hans Bengtsson and George Atkinson have written a definitive book on orienteering which is published by the Stephen Greene Press.

SANDSHOEING IN SUMMER

What happens after all the snow has melted? Well — you can try sandshoeing. We guess it all began in June of 1977 in front of the Hotel del Coronado on the beach at San Diego where a thousand yard triangular course was marked out with trash cans. The San Diego Mountain Rescue Team challenged any and all members of the California, Oregon, or Washington search and rescue teams and it was called the Snowshoe Thompson race. John Wehbring writes, "I still have a picture of the start, people dressed in everything from expedition down jackets, helmets, and goggles to bathing suits ... Most interesting were the snowshoes. I wore my standard wooden bearpaws, while some of the others wore the aluminum and nylon rigs that are popular here in California. Others wore the plastic bearpaws or fashioned 'snowshoes' from garbage can lids, wood

Rose Mary Gabriel, 46-year-old mother of seven and grandmother of nine, adjusts her snowshoes while practicing for the upcoming Yukon Jack World Snowshoe Championship, an 83-mile race held in Wisconsin. PALM PHOTO

slats, or even cardboard. You understand that there was no standards committee to rule on authenticity.'' He goes on to say that the race was only held once but that they may try it again. Members of the United States Snowshoe Association have also tried sandshoeing on the "Million Dollar Beach" of Lake George, New York. If you think you might like to try sandshoeing, we'd advise that you use an old run-down pair of snowshoes, as they will certainly take a beating in the sand.

MAKING YOUR OWN

Since the appearance of the first edition of *The Snowshoe Book* a number of people have asked us how they could learn to make their own snowshoes. As a result, we thought we would prepare a new chapter for this revised edition specifically on the technique and processes involved in the home manufacture of snowshoes.

To begin we should say that we undertake this chapter with some trepidation as we have not had a great deal of experience in this line. However, we have consulted with various skilled snowshoe craftsmen and have labored hard over several pairs of home-crafted snowshoes of our own, and now feel that the information we offer here should provide a good foundation for those who wish to take the time and pains to build snowshoes themselves.

A great advantage in any craft is to watch skilled craftsmen at work. We have had that opportunity with snowshoe making and remember with pleasure how we admired the skill and nimble fingers of lacers at work; one using a hook in Wallingford, Vermont, and another using a needle in Village Huron, Quebec. If you would like to share this same experience, why not try to get to Place Bonaventure in downtown Montreal about three weeks before Christmas each year where there is a special demonstration of snowshoe making as a small part of many other Canadian crafts exhibits sponsored by SMAQ (Salon Métiers Art Québec). These interesting exhibits have been held annually for twelve years. Another approach for visual instruction in snowshoe making would be to contact the Trust for Native American Cultures and Crafts at Box 199, Greenville, New Hampshire, 03048. The Trust has been making videotapes, including some lengthy, detailed versions, designed for serious craftsmen.

Later in the chapter we will say something about putting together emergency snowshoes, or what we call "half-hour" snowshoes. This will expand the material given in the "Something Out of Nothing" section on page 72 about expedient methods for hasty snowshoe construction. But for now let's get right to the more difficult matter at hand.

Making regular snowshoes will take considerably longer than half an hour. Warren Asa, writing on the subject in the Winter, 1971 issue of the *Hosteler* (magazine of the American Youth Hostels organization), says that it takes about ten hours of working time to make a pair of Michigan style snowshoes. While this may have been true for him, we found that making snowshoes from scratch requires quite a bit more time, and especially for the first pair when one has to add the time spent scouting up materials and tools. But, since we presume that

SUGGESTED LIST OF TOOLS AND EQUIPMENT FOR MAKING SNOWSHOES

Axe, single-bitted.

Bow saw with 36" blade.

Two steel wedges, about 4 pounds each.

Maul for driving wedges.

Drawknife.

Drawshave or Jack plane.

Shaving horse [optional].

Six or more C-clamps.

Handsaw with crosscut teeth [optional].

Steaming rig.

Two bending jigs.

Cowhide from a full-grown beast.

Twelve-gallon or more capacity water tub.

Plenty of clean water.

Two pecks of dry hardwood ashes.

Burlap sacking and twine for bundling the hide.

Pole, sawhorses, etc. for "graining" the hide.

Drying rack for rawhide [optional: it can just hang over the pole].

Drill. 1/4" bit with nibs for cutting into wood.

Chisel with 1/2" bit.

Router [optional: to replace above two tools].

Sandpaper, medium and fine grit.

Circle for cutting rawhide into thongs [12" or 14" bowl: or a pair of compasses].

Waterproof marker.

Sharp knife set with gage for stripping out thongs.

Lacer's hook or needle.

Plenty of enthusiasm and patience.

BILL OF MATERIALS FOR MAKING ONE PAIR OF OJIBWA STYLE SNOWSHOES _____
(approximately 10 1/2″ wide by 52″ long)

Eight strips of air-dried white ash wood — 3/4″ square by 54″ long, tapered to 3/4″ by 1/2″ about 3″ back from tips. Note: the extra pieces are in case of breakage during bending.

Four ash crossbars — two of them 1/4″ by 1″ by 10″, two of them 1/4″ by 1″ by 7″.

Thirteen yards of rawhide [babiche] strips 5′ to 7′ long by 3/8″ wide to lace the center section. An additional thirteen yards of 1/4″-wide strips to lace the toe and heel sections.

Eight rivets and washers. 1/4″ by 2″.

One pint of polyurethane varnish.

Two bindings.

anyone bent on making snowshoes is doing it for the sheer enjoyment of recreating an ancient craft, or as an experiment or challenge of some sort, the time element should not be that important. Just keep in mind that, if you do undertake making your own snowshoes, you will find it's a lengthy process from beginning to end and requires real dedication.

Let's assume that your first pair of snowshoes is to be made by the old method of using wood and rawhide (also known as *babiche*). The time to begin is in the spring just after the snow has left the ground. This will allow ample time to get them finished for the next winter's use.

Having set the rough time frame, we would suggest familiarizing yourself with the bill of materials and suggested tool and equipment list given here. These will give you a good idea of what you will need and a rough idea of the game plan.

THE BABICHE

The first step is to get the rawhide. It is possible to buy rawhide ready to use, but if you plan to be a purist and start from scratch, you will want to get a fresh cowhide at a slaughterhouse. Cowhide makes excellent babiche and is comparatively easy to obtain. Ask the butcher to take some pains in removing the bits and pieces of flesh and fat from the inner surface as this material comes off much more easily when the hide is warm. The cost of such a skin will be about ten dollars but be prepared to find considerable variation. Sometimes you can even get one for no charge.

Other types of skins which have been used for snowshoe rawhide are: moose, caribou, deer, seal, beaver, and bear. There is an interesting article by J.A. Burgesse on the subject of babiche and primitive snowshoe making in the March, 1941, issue of *The Beaver* (the journal of the Hudson's Bay Company). For greatest ease of operation, your rawhide preparation factory should be set up close to a good source of clean water; you will need a tub with at least a twelve-gallon capacity. The first step is to put the green cowhide in the tub, filling the tub with enough water to cover the hide completely. Weight the hide with stones to keep it under the surface of the water. Cover the tub to keep out inquisitive animals and let the hide soak for a couple of days.

THE FRAME STOCK

While the hide soaks is the time to procure the wood for the frames. The authors happen to be in the enviable position of having ample woodlands at our disposal but we realize that most people cannot just go out in the forest, select a prime tree and cut it. If you do not have access to your own woods, there are several alternatives open. The necessary wood can be purchased or arrangements can be made with a forest owner. Let's assume you can make proper arrangements with a woodlot owner; the next step is a pleasant excursion to look for a "Snowshoe Tree."

The "Snowshoe Tree"

All of the following trees (and probably others we have not heard of) have been used for making snowshoe frames:

Quaking Aspen (*Populus tremuloides*)
Paper Birch (*Betula papyrifera*)
Yellow Birch (*Betula alleghaniensis*)
American Elm (*Ulmus americana*)
Slippery Elm (*Ulmus rubra*)
Shagbark Hickory (*Carya ovata*)
Red Maple (*Acer rubrum*)
Sugar Maple (*Acer saccharum*)
Northern Red Oak (*Quercus rubra*)
Black Spruce (*Picea mariana*)
Red Spruce (*Picea rubens*)
White Spruce (*Picea glauca*)
Black Willow (*Salix nigra*)

However, the best snowshoe frames are made from the wood of the ash tree. Of the sixteen varieties of ash trees, five may be considered suitable for snowshoe making. These are the white, black, green, blue, and Oregon ash. The latter occurs naturally only in the states of Washington, Oregon, and California, and in the Province of British Columbia. White ash (*Fraxinus americana*) and black ash (*Fraxinus nigra*) are fairly common in the northeastern United States, around the Great Lakes district, and also in the southeastern Canadian provinces.

Most skilled snowshoe makers would agree that the white ash is the "Lord of the Snowshoe Trees" as the wood is very tough, shock resistant, and relatively easy to bend after it has been steamed. White ash is sometimes called Biltmore ash. Look for the white ash on upland sites where the soil is well drained. It seldom grows in pure stands and is most often found growing amongst the Eastern White Pine, Northern Red Oak, White Oak, Sugar Maple, Red Maple, Yellow Birch, American Beech, Black Cherry, American Basswood, Eastern Hemlock, American Elm, and Yellow Poplar.

Black ash is also much used for snowshoe frames, particularly in Wisconsin and Minnesota. This tree can tolerate wetter growing conditions. It is also called brown, basket, hoop, swamp, and water ash.

As the diagram shows, the bark of the ash is gray with rather deep furrows separated by narrow interlacing ridges. The leaves are compound. If you are looking for ash trees before the leaves have appeared, check the branches. Characteristically, the branches grow exactly opposite each other almost at right angles from the stem making the sign of the cross. For those who might need a short course in tree identification we can certainly recommend the little booklet prepared by the U.S. Forest Service: *Important Trees of Eastern Forests and Trees of North America: A Golden Field Guide* by C. Frank Brockman. It has fine illustrations and is easy to use.

Parts of the ash tree.

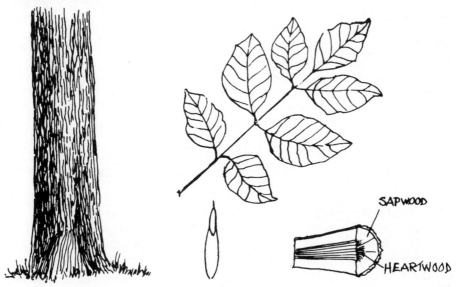

SAPWOOD

HEARTWOOD

Any tree that's to be used for making snowshoe frames must be straight, free from imperfections, and with no branches to a height of about fifteen or twenty feet. The bark can sometimes be used as an indicator of whether or not the wood is straight grained. If the furrowed bark on the trees runs in vertical lines evenly, the chances are good that the wood will split with a minimum of twisting. The diameter of the tree near the base should be six to ten inches. Anything much larger will be awkward to handle, especially as most people don't own log skidding equipment.

FELLING

After locating and obtaining permission to take the snowshoe tree, the next step is to cut it down. In cutting a tree it is much better for two people to work together. Working this way makes it both easier and safer.

Before beginning the cut it is wise to check the lean of the tree. This will affect the line of fall and your decision as to where best to fell the tree. Obviously, if a tree leans one way or another, one has to account for this in planning where to fell it, to avoid binding the saw in the cut and other complications.

Once the line of fall is determined, cut a notch in the tree near the base on the side where you wish the tree to fall. The notch, or undercut, should be as near horizontal as possible and about one quarter way through the tree. The best way to start the notch is to make one cut for the bottom edge with the saw and then chop out the rest of the notch, or scarf, with the axe.

Begin the next saw cut or backcut on the side of the tree opposite the notch and just slightly above the lower edge of the scarf. A bow saw, when used by two persons pulling alternately, works very nicely for this. Stand clear of the tree as it is about to fall and watch above for flying limbs, often called "widow-makers" and with good reason. A word to the wise: the expert felling of trees is an art; if you are a beginner in this field, a few minutes spent with a good woodsman's manual (for instance, the "Felling" chapter in Rockwell Stephen's *One Man's Forest*) might save you a lot of headaches.

Once the tree is down, using the axe, cut off all the limbs close to the trunk of the tree. Be sure to save as much of this limb wood as possible since it can be used later to fire up the steaming apparatus. Wood of the ash tree makes a nice hot fire and burns well even when green.

Snowshoe	Projected size	Length of bolt
Green Mtn. Bearpaw	10″ × 36″	should be 87″
Standard Bearpaw	12″ × 30″	should be 80″
Michigan	12″ × 42″	should be 94″
Alaskan Trail	10″ × 56″	should be 119″
Ojibwa	10″ × 48″	should be 54″

"Getting Out" the Stock

Commercial snowshoe makers use sawed lumber in getting out frame stock, but the home snowshoe maker will probably find that it is best to work the wood to correct size by first sawing off the proper length bolts, then by splitting, hewing, and shaving. Ash splits very nicely and all that will be needed for this is a couple of steel wedges and a maul to drive them with. (Don't be tempted to use the head of the axe to drive wedges — it's very hard on the axe.)

CUTTING THE BOLTS

Before deciding how long to cut the rough bolts to be used for the frames from the main log, you must have determined which type of snowshoe you wish to make. Refer back to pages 17 through 20 for a description of several popular models. The table below indicates how long to cut the bolts for five snowshoe styles and allows a bit extra for trimming the ends later.

If you wish to make snowshoes other than the styles given in the table, you will need to obtain a snowshoe to use as a pattern. To find the correct length for the unbent frame, just measure around the perimeter of the model snowshoe with a tape ruler and add an inch or so.

Once the bolts are cut is a good time to check the sawed ends to determine the number of annual growth rings. The best ash wood for making snowshoe frames has from twelve to fifteen annual growth rings per inch. If there are more, the frames will be difficult to bend and will not be as strong.

SPLITTING

When the bolt has been sawed to the correct length and checked for suitability, the bolt is split. To do this, place one of the wedges *exactly* in the center of the sawed off end. To get the best results the split should begin at the end of the bolt that was nearest the top of the tree. Drive the wedge in with the maul; in most cases the bolt of ash wood will split cleanly with just one wedge needed. If the split is not completed with the first wedge, a second can be placed along the crack to finish the job; or in many cases a considered blow with the axe will accomplish the same results. After the bolt has been split, check the split surface for straightness of grain. This should not diverge more than one inch in every fifteen inches.

Next is a good time to peel off the bark. If you are doing this work in the springtime you will find that the bark peels off readily. At other times of the year it may be necessary to use a drawknife to get the bark off. The bark must go as it is of no use at all, except possibly as fuel when it is dry. With the bark off, you can see the outer surface of the sapwood and can examine it closely for signs of small knots that might have been covered by the bark.

Cut and split several bolts of wood in this manner, checking each for the qualities mentioned above. Select out the best of the split halves and quarter them, using the wedge and maul as before. A bolt that is about ten inches in

Using the drawknife to strip the bark from the bolt.

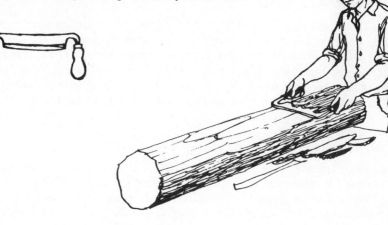

diameter can be split once again thus giving eight pieces. It is much more difficult to get good splits from bolts that are smaller in diameter so only split those into quarters.

All of this work can be done right where the tree was cut. Reducing the size of the pieces to be carried back to the workshop eases the chore. A four-foot long bolt of freshly cut white ash six inches in diameter at the large end weighs in at fifty pounds or so. Before leaving the area, salvage as much of the tree as possible to use as firewood; then assemble the materials gathered thus far at the place where you will finish shaving the frames down to size and where the steaming and bending will be done.

HEWING

The next step is to hew the frame stock down to size—in this case, a strip about an inch and a half wide by an inch and a half high. When the wood is newly cut, we have found it works best to use a very sharp axe. Working around the sapwood, carefully hew off most of the heartwood to roughly shape the frame stock. This can be done by eye, or if you don't trust your eye, use a straightedge to check the work from time to time. Hew slowly and deliberately, as a false stroke with the axe can ruin the whole job. Watch for the way the grain of the wood runs and always hew or shave with the grain, not against it. Never cut into the sapwood as this is the most valuable part of the stick and will form the outer edge of the snowshoe frame.

Shorter sticks can be hewed by holding the pieces in an upright position on a chopping block with one hand while striking the axe with the other. Hold the axe handle about midway. Longer pieces will need to be placed horizontally on a couple of blocks of wood laid on the ground with one end of the stick resting against a firm surface to keep it from slipping back each time the axe strikes.

Using an axe to hew and shape a piece of frame stock while a good working steamer gets hot in the foreground. Normally, since the hewed frame stock must dry before using, these steps would not occur concurrently. BRIDGE HILL STUDIO PHOTO

This work can be done in a kneeling position. If you have never done much work with an axe before, you will come to appreciate the skills of the old-time woodsman.

SHAVING

Once the hewing is done the frame stock will have to be shaved down to finished size by using first a drawknife and then a drawshave. The drawknife is a two-handled tool with a single beveled cutting edge running between the handles at right angles and on the same plane (see diagram). It is worked by pulling it towards the operator while the material is clamped to a bench.

There is a special kind of bench for this work called a shaving horse. It is described in Alex W. Bealer's *Old Ways of Working Wood* (Barre Publishers, 1972). There is also a picture of a shaving horse and other valuable information on the old crafts in *The Foxfire Book* (Doubleday Anchor Books, 1972). However, since we assume that most people attempting to make snowshoes will not wish to go to the extra work of making a shaving horse, we advise that the work simply be clamped to a bench while being shaved. C-clamps or carpenters' hand screws can be used for this. The clamps will also be needed later to hold the bent frames on the jigs after they have been steamed.

When the frame stock has been shaved down to a little over three-quarters by three-quarters inches, finish the shaving to a final dimension of three-quarter-inches square with the drawshave or a jack or block plane. A drawshave (also see diagram) is similar to a drawknife except that its blade projects through a slot in the body of the tool so that a shaving of controlled thickness can be taken off. As with a plane, the thickness of the shaving can be regulated by moving the blade in or out and clamping it in the desired position. With shaving as with hewing, never cut into the sapwood. Any slight imperfections there can be smoothed off later after the frame has been steamed and bent.

All snowshoe frames require that additional wood be shaved out to facilitate bending. The Ojibwa frame which is in two pieces for each snowshoe is tapered

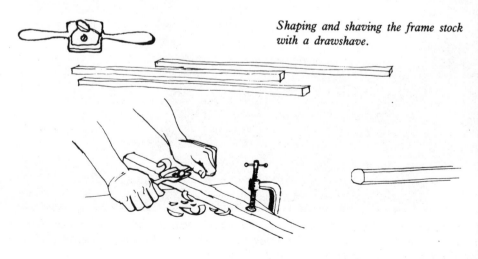

Shaping and shaving the frame stock with a drawshave.

smoothly down to a half inch by three quarters of an inch at either end where the toe and tail are fixed together. Other styles have some wood removed from the inner edge at the place where the toe bend comes. Additionally, bearpaw styles are tapered down at the tail so that when bent, the tail portion of the frame will be of equal width throughout where the ends overlap. Here again consult the diagram of your chosen snowshoe design, or better still, the real thing.

DRYING

Make up enough finished stock to have extra pieces on hand at the time the frames are bent as about one in five break when the wood is forced into the unnatural position of a snowshoe frame. When you have sufficient stock ready, the pieces should be put aside in a cool, dry place to season in the air. Some snowshoe makers advise going right ahead with the steaming and bending, but we think it is best to allow the stock to air dry. A month will bring the wood down to about an ideal twenty per cent moisture content. Wood set aside to dry should be laid horizontally with the longer pieces supported in the middle to avoid sagging. Allow plenty of room for air circulation by putting thin strips of wood crosswise between layers.

We figure that the work involved in getting this much of the job done — the cutting, splitting, hewing, and shaping — will take a full day under ideal conditions and more likely two or three days, and this assuming that only one or two pair of snowshoes are going to be made.

BACK TO THE BABICHE

The interlude while the shaped frame stock dries can be used to advantage to finish the babiche, to make up the bending jigs, and to put together some sort of steam generating apparatus.

If the hide was put to soak in clear water as suggested earlier, it should be fully softened and ready for the next step after two or three days. When ready, pull the hide out of the tub and lay it flat on the ground with the flesh side up. Using a sharp knife, *carefully* cut loose any remaining bits of fat and meat. Then trim off the edges of the hides so that it is roughly rectangular. This will mean cutting off the portions which formerly covered the legs, and the soft, thin, belly section.

Once the hide is trimmed, turn the hide over so the hair side is up and cover the hair liberally with hardwood ashes. Pour enough water on the ashes to make a thick paste and work it into the hair thoroughly with a stick. Don't use your hands for this, as the caustic action released by wood ashes being moistened with water can be very hard on your skin. Roll up the hide with the hair side in and tie the bundle up tightly. Put it in a damp, cool place, perhaps on the earthen floor of a cellar. Cover it with wet burlap and let it stay there for three or four days. Be prepared for a struggle — a sopping wet cowhide at this stage will weigh close to sixty pounds.

MAKING THE JIG

While the lye in the ashes is loosening the hair from the hide is a good time to be thinking about the design of the bending jig and planning the steam generator for softening the wood.

The easiest sort of jig to make would be the type for flat bearpaw snowshoes with no upturn at the toes (see diagram). An old plank of softwood two inches thick by twelve inches wide and at least five feet long will serve the purpose. Take the snowshoe you intend to duplicate and cut out a cardboard pattern to fit the inside of the frame; or use the snowshoe itself as the pattern. Hold the pattern or the snowshoe on the plank, and using a soft lead pencil, scribe along the edge of the pattern or the *inside* edge of the snowshoe frame so that the outline is transferred to the plank. Using a handsaw you can cut off most of the surplus wood: then finish the job by hewing with the axe, drawknife and block plane until the entire jig has a smooth outline.

The next step is to prepare the holes for the clamps. To do this, find some cast-off pieces of iron waterpipe with at least a one-inch inside diameter; then, with a hacksaw cut off about twenty-four lengths of the same thickness as the bending jig. The reason for the pipe is that it acts as reinforcement when the clamps are tightened.

Next, select a wood-boring auger the correct size to cut a hole equal to the outside diameter of the iron pipe. Bore a number of holes about one and one half inches in from the edge of the bending jig. The holes should be placed where there will be the most bending tension. The primary hole will be at the front, or toe, end of the jig. Fit the pieces of iron pipe into the holes, securing them in place with glue if they are a bit loose. Normally, one jig is required for each snowshoe you plan to make. We have considered trying to bend a *pair* of flat bearpaw snowshoes on a single jig but haven't gotten around to doing this yet.

Jig Variations

Different jigs are necessary for bending snowshoes with upturn at the toes. These require a shaped block to hold the bent toe plus the right amount of

A bearpaw frame on its jig with the clamps in place.

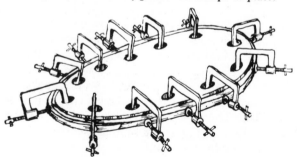

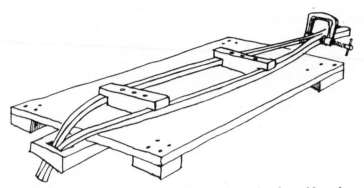

The jig for an Ojibwa snowshoe with the frame in place. Note the additional piece affixed to the front to hold the tip in position while it dries.

upturn. A variation on the hole and clamp variety of jig we have described would be a jig with blocks of wood nailed and glued in place along the inner outline of the snowshoe pattern. Yet another variation would be a jig made of a plank with the toe end shaped to give the right amount of upturn of Ojibwa style snowshoes (see diagram). A piece of board is affixed to the underside of the jig with a hole exactly in the center of this board large enough to receive the joined tips of this style. And two spreaders are nailed to the jig at about the place where the front and rear crossbars will later be placed. This is very well described in Ben Hunt's *Big Indian Craft Book* (Bruce Publishing Company, 1945).

ONCE AGAIN THE BABICHE

Cleaning

With the jig completed, attention can be turned back to the babiche. Three or four days of curing should loosen the hair from the hide enough so it can be scraped off. Open the bundle and try a section. If the hair is still tight, add some more ashes and water and bundle the skin up again for another day or so. After the hair has loosened sufficiently take the bundle outside, open it up, and rinse off the wood ashes, as well as any hair that is willing to come along. A good stream of water from a hose is just right to thoroughly cleanse the hide. When thoroughly rinsed hang the hide over a long pole suspended between two sawhorses.

Graining

The next step is called "graining." For this you can use the same drawknife that was used for shaving the wood off the snowshoe frames, only with a big difference. This time the back, blunt edge of the drawknife is used and instead of pulling it towards you, you push it away from you over the hide against the direction of the hair—this to clean off the hair and the scarf skin or epidermis.

123

This job takes lots of elbow grease. There are special tools made for graining babiche, but we think the drawknife will work well enough for only one or two hides. Scrape both sides of the skin carefully, rinsing it from time to time to keep it moist and to wash off the debris.

A cold, wet and rainy day is just the time for this sort of job. Wear a pair of rubber boots and waterproof overalls so you can sit astraddle the pole and hold the hide to keep it from slipping away as you scrape, scrape, scrape. If you get tired just put the hide back in the tub and cover it with fresh water until you have recovered your energy for another scraping bout. This is the type of work that is best to do in early spring before the weather gets warm enough to turn the hide putrid and make your job even more difficult.

Drying

When the scraping sessions are finished, you will need a rack for drying the hide. For this, use four poles lashed tightly together at each corner to form a rectangle about six inches larger than the size of the hide. Allow two of the poles to be long enough to keep the frame well away from the ground when the drying begins. When the hide has been scraped smooth and clean on both sides, lay it on the ground and cut a series of slots near the edge on all four sides and about eight to ten inches apart. Lash the hide to the drying frame so that it is quite tight and put the frame on end in a shady place, perhaps against a building or some trees, where the breeze can blow on it to dry it thoroughly. If a spot can be found out of the reach of inquiring animals so much the better.

Check the lashing from time to time and tighten or loosen it as may be required. Rather soon it will be dry and hard as a board and you will see how babiche in this state could have been very effective when used by warring Indians as a shield to deflect enemy arrows. As long as the hide remains dry it will last indefinitely and could be stored in any sheltered place out of the reach of gnawing rodents.

THE STEAMER

The steam generator is the next order of business. We have used an old cast-iron pig-feeding trough covered with a section of old sheet-iron roofing with success. The trough, where the frame stock will be steamed, is supported on stones and a fire built under and around it to bring the water in the trough to a boil. Another possibility would be to get an old water heater tank at the dump. Take it to someone who has oxy-acetylene gas cutting and welding equipment. Have one end cut off square with the cutting torch and then have the tank cut in half lengthwise. The cut ends welded together will provide a steaming tank about ten feet long.

Mr. Richard L. Floyd of Ely, Minnesota, who has made many pair of snowshoes as a hobby, says that his steaming equipment is ". . . simply a ten foot length of six inch pipe with one end welded shut. I elevate the open end

Another type of steamer improvised from an old milk can and several lengths of stovepipe insulated with burlap sacks. OSGOOD PHOTO

about five feet off the ground, fill the pipe with water, light a fire under the closed end and I'm in business." If you can tap a steam line conveniently you could direct the steam into a length of stove pipe which has the open end stuffed loosely with rags. We have even thought that snowshoe frames could be steamed on top of a maple syrup evaporator during the sugaring season. There are many possibilities that could be improvised out of available materials. The objective in any case is to thoroughly impregnate the wood with plenty of moist heat.

FABRICATING THE FRAMES

Bending

The moment of truth comes on steaming and bending day when likely you will find that some of the labor you expended on hewing and shaving the frame stock was for naught. Often some of the wood breaks while being bent; so be prepared for some disappointments.

First, fire up your steamer. Put the frame stock itself right in the tank and then keep the apparatus going full tilt for at least two hours before trying to bend any of the stock. Being careful to use heavy gloves when taking the frame stock out of the steam chest, try each piece for "bendability." When a piece seems supple enough, clamp it to the jig made for it at the point where the toe of the snowshoe will be, then bend the rest of it right around and clamp as necessary. (Obviously, this procedure changes to accommodate the different snowshoe patterns; the bearpaw requiring one solid piece of stock bent from the middle, the Ojibwa two separate pieces, etc.) Work quickly. It's good to have a helper at this stage.

In several of the snowshoe factories we have visited we have noticed that the workers put a band of flexible metal strapping on the tip section with gripper pliers to give some reinforcement to that critical point when the bend is made.

Frames bent and clamped to the jigs should be left in place for at least a week; then they may be removed and allowed to dry further for two weeks more. During this second drying stage it will be important to place some wooden spreaders inside the frame to help hold the shape. If, by this time, the season has moved along into summer, you might want to put the frames in the attic where they will dry all the more quickly up under the roof.

Fitting the Crossbars

While the frames dry would be a good time to whittle out the crossbars. Each pair of the snowshoe styles we have been discussing requires a total of four crossbars; these can be made out of the same wood the frame stock came from. Each crossbar will be about one and one-half inches wide by one-quarter inch thick with the length to be determined by just where the crossbar fits on the frame.

Fitting in the crossbars can be done in several ways. If you are using a finished snowshoe for a model, you can measure the model and use those measurements to find the location for the crossbars on the new snowshoes. Another method is to balance the new frame horizontally across a straightedge and then lay on the crossbars in their approximate positions about fifteen to seventeen inches apart. Move them until the snowshoe frame is slightly tail-heavy and mark the location of the crossbars in the frame with a pencil. This will indicate where the mortices are to be cut in.

Professional snowshoe makers put the mortices (a mortice, by the way, is nothing but a cabinetmaker's term for a slot) in with a power tool called a router. The same thing can be done with a hand drill and a chisel. Whether a power router is used or hand tools, the mortices should be carefully cut in to the dimension of one inch long, one-quarter inch deep by one-quarter inch wide. The ends of the crossbars can then be very carefully shaved down to fit the mortices.

Before the crossbars are put in place the ends of the frames are secured either with rivets or rawhide. The Ojibwa snowshoes have to be joind at both toes and tails while, as we have seen, the other models are only joined at the tails. In either case, holes will have to be made to receive rivets or rawhide (see diagram). The same quarter-inch drill that was used to make the mortices can do this job too. After the frames have been joined together, they can be sprung apart slightly and the crossbars slipped in place. No glue is needed.

Drilling the Lace Holes

Before you put the drill away plan to make the holes to be used for lacing the toe and heel sections. At this point, rather than try to deal with all the various, and rather complex, lacing patterns possible, we'll restrict our explanation to one type of snowshoe, the Ojibwa. The diagrams show very clearly where the holes are to be drilled. When drilling the holes clamp a piece of softwood to the underside directly below where the drill enters. This will avoid unwanted splintering. A fine touch would be to countersink each hole slightly. Beyond this, Mr. Floyd advises cutting a groove between holes as added protection to the lacing of the toe and heel sections. The final step before the lacing begins is to sand down any imperfections on the frame and carefully to take off all sharp edges that might chafe the lacing.

THE LACING

To prepare the dried babiche for cutting into lacing thongs first smooth it with sandpaper or pumice stone. Then, check the dry rawhide over for uneven spots and note where the hide is of best quality. Turn a twelve- or fourteen-inch mixing bowl upside down over the good spots on the hide and trace a circle with an indelible marker around every place where the hide can be used.

At this point, put the hide back in warm water to soak again for a while. Even

Here two well-steamed pieces of frame stock are bent to fit an Ojibwa jig. Note how the center pieces are fitted around the stretchers. BRIDGE HILL STUDIO PHOTOS

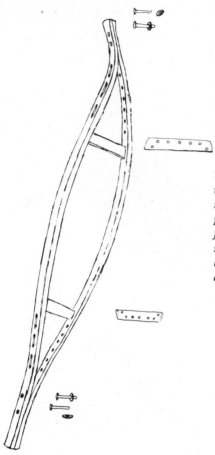

This diagram shows where the two pieces making the tip and tail of the Ojibwa frame should be riveted together, as well as where to place the crossbars and where to drill the holes for the toe and heel lacing. The toe crossbar should be 10 inches wide, while the heel crossbar should be 7 inches. Note that the crossbars are also drilled for lacing holes.

with this soaking the hide will likely still be stiff, you will probably have to cover it with burlap or other rags soaked in warm water to soften it enough to cut around the circles. After cutting, soak the circular sections a bit more until they are quite flexible, but not too soft to slice out the lacing material.

Lacing material three-eighths of an inch wide is best for center section lacing. A quarter of an inch or slightly less is good for toe and heel lacing. You will find that the lacing shrinks a bit on drying. It shrinks both in width, thickness and length. There is also considerable variation in the hide thickness depending on where it had been on the animal. Skin on the back is much thicker than belly hide. While the latter would be all right for lacing toe and heel sections, it would be far too flimsy for lacing the center sections. Keep these things in mind while cutting up your babiche and sorting out the lacing thongs.

Cutting the Thongs

A rather simple way of making the lacing thongs is to drive a small nail part way into the workbench and press the tip of a *very sharp* knife into the bench three-eighths of an inch away from the nail with the blade slanting just slightly backwards.

Then, with another sharp knife cut along the circumference of a circle of babiche to provide a short starting strip. Fit this strip between the knife blade and the nail on the bench and then, by pulling on the starter strip, force the uncut hide against the cutting edge of the knife to get fairly long strips of lacing material as the circular piece of hide goes round and round until the center is reached. Aim for strips as long as possible.

To make the narrower quarter-inch strips, just set the knife closer to the nail and start again. It takes a bit of practice to get just the right slant on the knife blade to make the lacing you want, but once things are set up properly it all goes rather quickly. If you intend to begin weaving the pattern on the frames right away, throw the newly cut strips of lacing into a pail of water; otherwise, you can let the lacing dry up again for storage.

LACING THE SHOES

The best way to learn to lace snowshoes would be as an apprentice to a master lacer. Lacking that opportunity, the next best way is to work from the diagrams that Grace Brigham has drawn for this chapter. She has simplified the traditional Ojibwa pattern somewhat to make the lacing easier.

We think it is easier to lace with babiche than with the new synthetics. When rawhide is wet it's very flexible and easy to cut. Lacing with rawhide is best done with lengths of from five to seven feet, splicing lengths together as needed.

Splicing

To make a splice in rawhide, cut a half-inch slit lengthwise of the thong in use, beginning the slit about a quarter-inch back from the end. Cut a corresponding slit in the thong which will be attached. Pass the end of the first piece through the slit in the piece to be attached and then draw the loose end of the new thong through the slit in the one being spliced into. One does not need too much tension; just draw it up rather snug. Later, when the rawhide dries, it will shrink nice and tight.

Lacing Aids

Some professional lacers have a special clamp to hold the snowshoe steady while they are working. Others grip the frame between the body and one arm but this takes a good deal of agility. We suggest that the frame be clamped to a firm surface at an angle of about seventy degrees thereby leaving both hands free. A convenient lacing tool is shaped like an oversized crochet hook. Some Indians use a bone needle with a hole in the middle and a blunt point at either end. These are great aids, with the lacing hook being easier to learn to use than the needle.

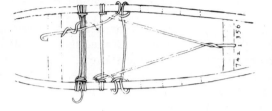

LACING AN OJIBWA SNOWSHOE Working from the upper left to lower right, and using 33 feet of 3/8th-inch cord, follow these diagrams to lace the center section of an Ojibwa snowshoe. It looks complicated but with patience and care this pattern should be mastered.

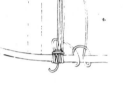

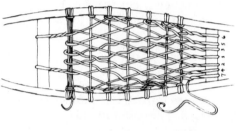

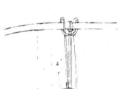

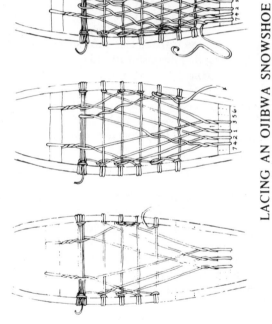

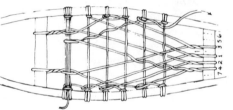

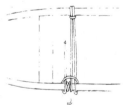

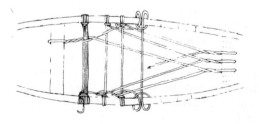

LACING AN OJIBWA SNOWSHOE

The Strategy

The lacing for the center section is done first. It is started on the left hand side of the frame about four and one-half inches down from the crossbar. The master or toe cord is the first part to be done. To complete the center section lacing, follow the diagrams. Any splicing in the center section should be done at the frame.

When the center section has been laced, it is set aside to dry overnight. The next day a reinforcing thong of babiche is wound around the toe or master cord and sometimes around the lengths that form the sides of the toe hole.

It doesn't matter in which order the toe and heel sections are laced. In order to help thread the babiche through the holes in the frame it is handy to take a piece of wire and double it over the end of the thong. Splices in toe and heel sections are not made at the frame. Here again follow the diagrams.

Let the completely laced snowshoes dry thoroughly and then give them a good coat of polyurethane varnish. The only thing left to do then is to make up some bindings. Some suggested binding patterns are given on pages 34 through 44. Rawhide for bindings can be made flexible by rubbing plenty of neatsfoot oil into the thongs when they are dry and then drawing the thongs back and forth over the edge of a board to make them supple.

Alternative Laces

We have gone to some length to explain as much as we could about preparing babiche so that those who wished to could make their own snowshoes as much along traditional lines as possible. However, we realize that some may wish to skip the rawhide step completely. Good lacing material can be purchased at any local hardware store in the form of one-eighth inch halyard weave nylon cord. This can be used very well to lace all three of the snowshoe sections; toe and heel as well as center section. In using nylon cord keep plenty of tension on it while lacing and keep splices or knots to a minimum. Flat weave nylon lacing material

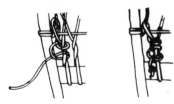

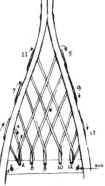

At top: the final tie-off pattern for the Ojibwa lacing pattern shown at left. At right: the pattern for the toe and heel sections of the Ojibwa is identical. Use 8 feet of 1/4-inch cord for each.

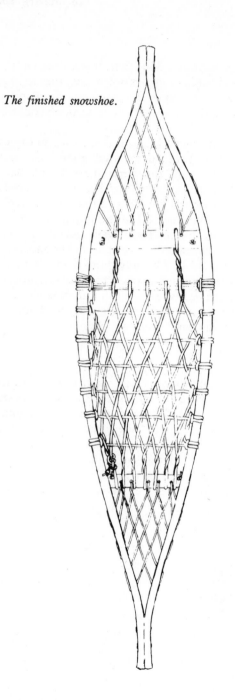

The finished snowshoe.

is very nice to use and is supplied in a number of the snowshoe making kits. Country Ways, Inc. (see our Snowshoe Makers List for full address) supplies this flat weave nylon by the yard, in precut amounts for various size frames, or by 500 yard spools. Write to them for prices.

Yet another substitute for rawhide is the metal mesh called hardware cloth. In February, 1929, *Popular Mechanics* magazine published an article giving complete directions for using this cloth for snowshoes. A reprint of this article can be purchased from them for one dollar by sending an order to: Popular Mechanics, X628 Snowshoes, 224 West 57th St., New York, New York, 10019.

USING A KIT

For budding snowshoe makers who would prefer not to start from scratch, there are kits available on the market. They come complete with all components, and full directions for assembly. Several U.S. snowshoe manufacturers offer kits for sale, but we have not seen any kits on the Canadian market. The average savings to be realized by putting together snowshoes from a kit based on 1979–1980 prices would be about sixteen dollars a pair. Country Ways, Inc. of Minnetonka, Minnesota, specializes in kits of all sorts for outdoor equipment. We have assembled one of their snowshoe kits and enjoyed the whole process very much. For others who might like to try assembling snowshoes from a kit we have noticed that these companies in addition to Country Ways, Inc. include snowshoe making kits in their catalogues: Black Forest Snowshoe Co., Early Winters, Ltd., Havlick Snowshoe Co., Vermont Tubbs (full addresses for these companies may be found in our Snowshoe Makers list). Some may enjoy reading an article about snowshoe making kits that appeared in the December, 1978, issue of *Mechanix Illustrated* magazine.

"HALF-HOUR" SNOWSHOES

As we indicated at the start, we do not want to close this new chapter on making your own snowshoes without some reference to what we call "half-hour" snowshoes. These are the type that might be used in an emergency situation and are not intended for long trips.

In the "Something Out of Nothing" section on page 72 we mentioned some facts about expedient methods for hasty snowshoe construction. Since that section was written, we have had the experience of a class in outdoor education composed of women students who actually made and used these simple snowshoes as part of their training. We call them "half-hour" snowshoes because this is how long it took these students to make them.

For each snowshoe these students broke off five to seven branches of the Jack Pine, selecting those branches with the most needles, each branch being about three feet long. Three branches were used for the base with the butts forming the toe of the snowshoe and the tips the tail. Since there is a natural bend to the limbs, this could be used to advantage to create a slight upturn to the snowshoes making them less likely to dig into the snow when worn. In addition to the three or four branches needed for the base of each snowshoe, a couple were added to form a rough pocket for the foot which was tied into this pocket in a position to make the snowshoe slightly tail heavy. The branches were tightly banded together with wire or twine. Anyone could follow this simple procedure to make emergency snowshoes. A good style of binding to use would be the Alaskan type shown on page 41.

The user might still find it better to take a turn around the tips, over the butt ends of the branches, and to pull back with some slight tension to create a bit more upturn. This would give the effect of trail-type snowshoes which are more effective in deep snow. This type of emergency equipment will give good service for trips of four to five miles. They have about half the flotation qualities of regular snowshoes.

Jack Pine (*Pinus banksiana*), the tree used for making the half-hour snowshoes described above, is quite a common tree in Canada and in the northernmost United States. Branches of other evergreen trees are also suitable. A prime quality is needed with plenty of needles to help provide good flotation in deep, soft snow.

The students, in their case, were careful to use trees on college land and avoid impairing the future growth of any tree. One might not be able to be quite so conscientious in an emergency situation but thought should be given to the proper conservation of growing things whenever possible. The time has passed when we can just go out into the forest and cut indiscriminately.

For those interested in more information along this line, William H. Bradfield has spent quite a bit of time studying emergency-type snowshoes. His article on the subject in the November, 1973, issue of *Field and Stream* magazine is worth reading. As we have done, he also cautions prudence in the use of the woodlands for gathering materials to make this type of snowshoe.

RESOURCE LIST |

Since the publication of the earlier editions of our book there has been a small yet significant increase in snowshoe reference material which we have tried to reflect in this list. In addition we have included entries for films, videotapes, and the locations of a few of the museum snowshoe collections in North America, hoping that this will make the list more useful to our readers.

BOOKS AND PERIODICALS

Appalachia. A periodical published by the Appalachian Mountain Club at 5 Joy St., Boston, MA 02108.

BAUER, Erwin A. *Cross-Country Skiing and Snowshoeing*. South Hackensack, NJ, Stoeger Pub. Co., 1975.

Beaver: Magazine of the North published at Hudson's Bay House, 77 Main St., Winnipeg, Manitoba, Canada R3C 2R1.

BECKET, Hugh W. *The Montreal Snow Shoe Club*. Montreal, Becket Bros., 1882.

CAMERON, Mary A. *Snow Tours in Washington*. rev. ed. Edmonds, WA, Signpost Book Co., 1979.

CARPENTIER, Paul. *La Raquette À Neige*. Sillery, P.Q., Les Éditions du Boreal Express, 1976.

COX, Gerald. *Wintersigns in the Snow*. With calligraphy by Kitty Weaver. Distributed by Country Ways, Inc. 3500 Hwy. 101 South, Minnetonka, MN 55353.

DAVIDSON, Daniel S. *Snowshoes*. Philadelphia, American Philosophical Society, 1937.

DRUMMOND, Thomas. *The Canadian Snowshoe*. Ottawa, J. Hope, 1916.

EVANS, Eric. *A Long Day's Journey Revisited*. In: *Sportscape*. Dec. 1982. (This article and the one following make interesting comparisons about snowshoeing over the course of 22 years)

EVANS, Robert J. *Winter Climb in New Hampshire*. In: *Summit*. Nov. 1959.

FINCH, Phillip. *Rigged For Silent Walking*. In: *Backpacker*. Aug.-Sep. 1981.

GILMAN, Roger B. *Snowshoes*. In: *Appalachia*. Dec. 1969.

GILPATRICK, Gil. *Building Snowshoes*. Yarmouth, ME, De Lorme Pub. Co., 1979.

HEILMAN, Carl E. *Snowshoe Making*. In: *Mother Earth News*. Nov.-Dec. 1981. (Single copy costs $3.00. Order issue no. 72 from Mother's Back Issues. 105 Stoney Mtn. Rd., Hendersonville, NC 28971)

KREPS, Elmer H. *Woodcraft*. rev. ed. Columbus, OH, A.R. Harding Pub. Co., 1978.

LORTIE, Gerard. *La Raquette*. Montreal, Éditions du Jour, 1972.

Making Snowshoes. "This and others in series prepared for Tanana Survival School which was conceived by the Tanana Chiefs in 1973 as a means of teaching young people the Athabaskan way of life." Available from Adult Literacy Laboratory, Anchorage Community College, Bldg. A, Rm. 207, 2533 Providence Drive, Anchorage, AK 99504.

MELLOR, Malcolm. *Avalanches.* Hanover, NH, Cold Regions Research Engineering Laboratory.

OSGOOD, William E. and Leslie J. Hurley. *La Raquette.* (Translation of the *Snowshoe Book* first published in 1971) Montréal, Les Éditions de L'Homme, 1974.

OSGOOD, Willam and Prater, Gene. *Snowshoes East.* In: *Backpacker.* Aug.-Sep. 1981.

PRATER, Gene. *How A Western Snowshoer Came To Respect Mt. Washington.* In: *Backpacker.* Feb-Mar. 1980.

————. *Snow Trails: Ski and Snowshoe Routes in the Cascades.* Seattle, WA, The Mountaineers, 1975.

————. *Snowshoeing.* Seattle, WA, The Mountaineers, 1974.

————. *Snowshoes West.* In: *Backpacker.* Aug.-Sep. 1981.

Répertoire des Sentiers de Randonnée au Québec. 2ième éd. Montreal, Sentiers Quebec, 1979.

ROBERTS, Harry. *Movin' On: Equipment and Techniques for Winter Hikers.* Boston, Stone Wall Press, 1977.

Salt Book, edited by Pamela Wood. Garden City, NY, Anchor Press/Doubleday, 1977. (Describes snowshoe making techniques of Walter York in Caratunk, ME in addition to other articles on country folk and country ways)

VAILLANCOURT, Henri. *Snowshoe Making.* (New text in preparation. Ready in 1983 or 1984.)

WOLFRAM, Gerry. *Walk Into Winter.* New York, Scribner, 1978. Toronto, J. Wiley, 1977.

FILMS AND VIDEOTAPES

Snowshoes/La Raquette. 1978, 15 mins., color, no narration. (Shows aspects of Montagnais life and craftsmanship. Part of How To Do It series.) Available from: Department of Indian and Northern Affairs, A/V Central Services, les Terrasses de la Chaudière, 19th floor, Hull, P.Q. Canada K1A OH4.

Snowshoeing. 1968, 12 mins., color, English narration. (Explains how the ungainly snowshoe was invented by the Indians long ago.) Available from: Marlin Motion Pictures, Ltd., 47 Lakeshore Road, East, Port Credit, Ont., Canada L5G 1C9.

Trust for Native American Cultures and Crafts. Box 199, Greenville, NH 03048. (The Trust produces broadcast quality documentary videotapes about traditional crafts and cultures of northern native peoples. Includes birchbark canoe and sealskin kayak making, hide tanning, the manufacture of various types of snowshoes, toboggans, sleds, tools, and skin and fur clothing.)

SNOWSHOE COLLECTIONS IN MUSEUMS

In process now is a computerized inventory of special collections in Canadian museums being prepared by the National Museum of Man. Ottawa, Ont., Canada K1A OM8. Phone (613) 996–9284.

The anthropological collection at the U.S. National Museum (Smithsonian) in Washington, D.C. would be a prime resource as would be the Museum of the American Indian and the American Museum of Natural History, both in New York City. Harvard's Peabody Museum of Archaeology and Ethnology has a collection of snowshoes, only a small part of which is on public display. So does the Chateau de Ramezay in Old Montreal. Many privately financed museums throughout North America have significant snowshoe collections which can be made available to the serious student for research. But we admonish our readers not to make casual requests of institutions which rely on very limited private funds and volunteer assistance.

NORTH AMERICAN SNOWSHOE MAKERS

Long ago, snowshoes were made by individuals for their own use according to time-honored styles peculiar to certain regions. Much depended on snow condition. Was it soft and powdery; or hard and crusty? Were the woodlands open; or full of "puckerbrush"? As time went on some particularly skilled snowshoe makers began to trade or sell their products, thus making the great transition from subsistence to commercial economics. We have heard that the first full-scale snowshoe manufacturing enterprise was that of Alanson Millen Dunham, Jr. at Norway, Maine, in 1862. The smaller snowshoe making enterprises still thrive here and there. Our list gives the names and addresses of several people who make and sell a dozen or so pair each year. Indeed we are aware of quite a few snowshoe makers that are purposely not included in the list because their product is sold directly in their own locality.

Research for compiling this listing took place early in 1980. We found that some of the snowshoe makers included in our earlier list have gone out of business while others have taken their places. Our new listing is quite a bit larger than the previous ones. This is a good sign, for the makers of snowshoes are one with the hewers of wood and the drawers of water — useful people in today's world.

In order to make this list more helpful we are adding some brief notes after the names and addresses describing general and particular information about their products. We have coded the general facts according to snowshoe styles as described in our chapter on selecting snowshoes:

M   Maine or Michigan.
O   Ojibwa.
W   Westover.
A   Alaskan or Trail.
B   Bearpaw or Beavertail.

Snowshoe nomenclature of course includes many more types of classification, but we felt it would be best to keep this coding as simple as possible. Since quite a few snowshoes are made of plastic material we have added (P) after the basic codes given above as a further aid.

Please note that most snowshoe makers usually offer several sizes within each style pattern. Also they almost invariably sell the bindings for the snowshoes in several patterns.

At first we thought we would try to include prices charged by the individual snowshoe makers, but we found that this would become practically worthless as an aid after only a very short time because of the current inflation rate. In general you will find forty dollars a pair at the lower and two hundred dollars as about the upper limit. Most snowshoes (without bindings) now sell between fifty and eighty dollars a pair. Beyond this we dare say no more.

INTRODUCTION TO UNITED STATES SNOWSHOE MAKERS LIST

In comparing the snowshoe production of the U.S. and Canada it is interesting to note that much of the current U.S. effort is devoted to the newer styles, which use aluminum and synthetics. Also the U.S. snowshoe makers often have kits available so people can assemble the snowshoes at home. This practice has not apparently found favor in Canada.

U.S. snowshoe makers producing traditional types of snowshoes using the wood frames and standard lacing procedures are having a difficult time meeting Canadian competition. The U.S. import tax on snowshoes is not sufficient to compensate for a Canadian subsidy paid to encourage Canadian industry.

UNITED STATES SNOWSHOE MAKERS

Black Forest Snowshoe Co.
P.O. Box 1007
Nevada City, CA 95959
   Phone (916) 265–3460

B. This company has been in business since 1962, and are pioneers of the aluminum frame snowshoes which can be purchased fully assembled or as a kit to do it yourself.

Country Ways, Inc.
3500 Highway 101 South
Minnetonka, MN 55343
   Phone (612) 473–4334

O. In addition to their snowshoe kits for home assembly, this company has kits for many other items useful for outdoorspeople.

Early Winters, Ltd.
110 Prefontaine South
Seattle, WA 98104
   Phone (206) 622–5203

B. Especially light aluminum frame snowshoes available as a kit or fully assembled.

Green's Custom Snowshoes
R.D. 1
Broadalbin, NY 12025

W. Mr. Green has been making snowshoes for over ten years. He uses the trade name "Northover."

Havlick Snowshoe Co.
P.O. Box 508
Gloversville, NY 12078
  Phone (518) 725-6175

M,W,B. Aluminum frame snowshoes available. Also kits for the Green Mtn. bearpaw style. Other products include ski and coat racks, white ash walking sticks, and firewood carriers. Also lightweight racing snowshoes.

Carl E. Heilman II
Box 213 A Rte 8
Brant Lake, NY 12815

M,O,A,B. Custom made snowshoes only on request needing four to six weeks for completion of an order. Mr. Heilman has designed a very light wood frame racing snowshoe he calls the "Catpaw."

Iverson Snowshoes, Inc.
Maple St. Box # 85
Shingleton, MI 49884
  Phone (906) 452-6370

M,W,A. Iverson Snowshoes have pioneered the use of nylon-reinforced Neoprene for webbing.

R. Merritt
R.R. 2 Box 186
Cohasset, MN 55721

M,A. Unusual, extra-long, Alaskan trail-type snowshoes. Also a special design of the Michigan style with sharp upturn at the nose. Mr. Merritt makes dog sleds as well. Only limited production.

Polar Equipment
12881 Foothill Lane
Saratoga, CA 95070
  Phone (408) 867-4576

Aluminum frame with built-in traction aids and innovative step-in, quick lock/quick release binding.

Prater Snowshoes
Route 1 Box 725
Ellensburg, WA 98926

Handcrafted snowshoes of aluminum tubing, coated nylon decking laced to the frames with polyurethane. Gene Prater is well known for his writings on snowshoeing as well as his unique approach to snowshoe designs. Sells only direct to individuals.

Seymour Supply Co.
Arlington, WI 53911

O. Mr. Seymour has a radical version of the traditional Ojibwa snowshoe built with the trapper in mind. Annual production limited to no more than a dozen pair.

Sherpa Snowshoe Co.
2222 W. Diversey Parkway
Chicago, IL 60647
    Phone (312) 772–6200

A widely-known aluminum frame snowshoe designed particularly with mountaineering in mind but useful on all terrain. Racing snowshoes also available.

The Snocraft Corp.
Oak Hill Plaza P.O. Box 487
Scarboro, ME 04074
    Phone (207) 883–3408

M,W,A,B. Also toboggans, sleds, white ash and rawhide furniture, the useful Burgess Hitch snowshoe binding, plus an unusual item called *Ski Skates*. This company will also re-lace snowshoe frames with rawhide or Neoprene.

Snow Valves
Ski Dynamics, Inc.
Bellport, NY 11713
    Phone (516) 286–9492

B(P) Molded in one piece from impact resistant polyolifin with forty-four movable snow valve flaps to improve weight carrying capacity.

Henri Vaillancourt
Box 199
Greenville, NH 03048

M,B. Mr. Vaillancourt builds his snowshoes on the traditional patterns as part of his work to perpetuate interest in the ancient crafts of the Indian and Inuit. A special feature is the lacing pattern in geometric figures seldom seen nowadays outside of museums.

Vermont Tubbs
Forest Dale, VT 05745
    Phone (802) 247–3414

M,A,B. Tubbs "alum-a-shoe" is a versatile addition to their line of traditional snowshoes. They also offer the X-C three-pin binding with two of their most popular models. Snowshoe kits for home assembly plus various articles of white ash and rawhide furniture.

Floyd Westover
R.D.1 Meco
Gloversville, NY 12078
    Phone (518) 725–0325

W. This man is the originator of the modified bearpaw style which has proved its worth.

Woodstream Corp.
P.O. Box 327
Lititz, PA 17543
    Phone (717) 626–2125

A(P) B(P)   Companion company of Woodstream — Canada which manufactures their special line of snowshoes made of supertough Lexan polycarbonte. A new feature is optional *Nordic norm* three-pin X-C ski bindings to be used with their snowshoes.

INTRODUCTION TO CANADIAN SNOWSHOE MAKERS LIST

In recent years we have heard that the Canadian government has made a special effort to support the snowshoe making (particularly by Indian groups) industry. Although we have not been able to verify the details of this subsidy, it does seem like an appropriate solution for the encouragement of this highly labor–intensive industry.

It is worth noting that perhaps the largest snowshoe manufacturing center in the world is located in the Quebec City suburb of Loretteville, the Indian Lorette or Village Huron where members of the Huron Tribe practice their ancient craft in a contemporary setting.

CANADIAN SNOWSHOE MAKERS

Avery and Sons
Box 339
Whitney, Ont.
K0J 2M0
   Phone (705) 637–2825

M,O.   Also make one-piece hardwood paddles.

Matthew Etiènne and Son
Oka Indian Reserve
Oka, P.Q.
J0N 1E0
   Phone (514) 479–8020

M,O,B.   Other products include chairs, lacrosse sticks, sleds, oars, paddles, axe, pick, sledge, hammer handles, cattle canes, and shepherd crooks.

Faber and Co., Inc.
180, Boul. de la Rivière
C.P. 100 Loretteville, P.Q.
G2B 3W6
   Phone (418) 842–8476

M,O,A,B.   This company has been in the same family for three generations. In addition to the usual snowshoes, they also make the special racing snowshoes. Another catalogue lists their line of canoes.

Les Industries Provinciales, Ltée. (IPL)
St-Damien, Bellechasse, P.Q.
G0R 2Y0
   Phone (418) 789–2880

M(P)   Also other plastic products for winter recreation including an interesting version of the old-time "jumper" sled.

Kabir Kouba Mfg. Enr.
(St-Charles River Mfg.)
Village Huron, P.Q.
G0A 4V0
   Phone (418) 842–3847

M,O,A,B.   Also mittens, moccasins, canoes, paddles.

Magline of Canada, Ltd.
Box 219 Renfrew, Ont.
K7V 4A3
   Phone (613) 432–5848

M.   Snowshoe frames are made of magnesium and laced with nylon-covered aircraft control cable. Although primarily sold for military use in Canada and abroad, they are also for sale to the civilian market only from the factory at the above address. A short but informative article about this unusual snowshoe company is to be found on page 44 of the April 7, 1980, issue of *Maclean's Magazine*.

Mistassini Snowshoe Factory
Baie du Poste, P.Q.
G0W 1C0

This company makes the Cree Traditional Snowshoes.

Pays Plat Mfg.
Via Rossport, Ont.
P0T 2R0
   ' Phone (807) 824–2541

O.   Authentic Indian-crafted snowshoes made from local resources.

Picard et Frère, Enr.
Village Huron, P.Q.
G0A 4V0
   Phone (418) 842–3865

M,O,A,B.   Their products include the special racing snowshoes and also the snowshoe moccasins.

Racking Akileine
Les Flots Bleu
Rue de Stade
Monaco

These plastic snowshoes most resemble the Swiss Army type shown on p. 26 . As far as we can tell, these are the only snowshoes made for civilian use outside of North America. Their products are distributed by La Beauté Française, Inc., 3405, Boul. Losch., St-Hubert, P.Q. Phone (514) 871–8873.

Raquettes Aigle Noir, Inc.
251, Boul. La Rivière
C.P. 250 Loretteville, P.Q.
G2A 1H2
   Phone (418) 842–4045

M,O,A,B.

Sports d'Hiver Huron, Enr.
Rue des Veterans
Village Huron, P.Q.
G0A 4V0
  Phone (418) 842–7984

M,O,A,B. This company was formerly known as Big Chief.

Sportspal Enterprises, Ltd.
P.O. Box 250 Callander, Ont.
P0H 1H0

M,O,B. Sportspal Enterprises has assumed manufacture and distribution of the famous Chestnut snowshoes that were made for many years in Fredericton and Oromocto, New Brunswick.

Torpedo, Ltée.
3677, Rue Lévis
Lac Mégantic, P.Q.
G6B 2H7
  Phone (819) 583–2478

M,A,B. Also make several sizes and types of toboggans, sleds and mini-skis. Torpedo does not sell retail.

Woodstream Corp.
P.O. Box 210
Niagara Falls, Ont.
L2E 6T3
  Phone (416) 357–3440

A(P) B(P) This Canadian affiliate of Woodstream–USA manufactures their special line of snowshoes made of supertough Lexan polycarbonate. A new feature is optional *Nordic norm* three-pin X-C ski bindings to be used with their snowshoes.

INDEX

Alaskan (snowshoe style), 19–20, 32, 116; *ill.* 20
Aleuts, 25
Algonquin (snowshoe style), 17; *ill.* 20
Aluminum snowshoes, 21; *ill.* 22
American Snowshoe Union, 9
Animal tracks, 66–68; *ill.* 66, 67, 68
Anorak, 48
Army binding, 34–37; *ill.* 36, 37
Avalanches, 77–85; *ill.* 81, 82

Babiche, 113–114, 121, 123–124, 127–133. *See also* Lacing, lacing patterns, rawhide
Balata binding, 36–37; *ill.* 37
Battle on Snowshoes, 6
Bearpaw (snowshoe style), 17, 18, 32, 116; *ill.* 18, 20, 23, 122
Beavertail (snowshoe style), 28; *ill.* 27
Bering Land Bridge, 2
Biathlon, 109
Bindings, 34–44. *See also* Army, Balata, Burgess, Heel control, Inner tube, Nylon strap, Squaw hitch
Boots, 45–47; *ill.* 46–47
Burgess binding, 36–37; *ill.* 36, 37
Bushwhacker (ski style), 28

Campfires, 94
Canadian Snowshoer's Union, 9
Clothing, 45–50
Clubs. *See* American Snowshoe Union, Canadian Snowshoer's Union, Montreal Snow Shoe Club, United States Snow Shoe Association
Conditioning, 102–103
Coureur de bois, 49
Crampons, 34–37, 50–52; *ill.* 36, 50–52
Crust spikes, 36–37, 50–52; *ill.* 36, 50–52

Daypacks, 92–93
Deer, 66–67; *ill.* 66
Delia, Joe, 37–38

Downhill travel techniques, 61–62; *ill.* 61

Edging, 59–60
Emergency equipment, 71–72, 135–136. *See also* Rescue techniques, Survival techniques
Equipment. *See* Bindings, Boots, Clothing, Crampons, Emergency equipment, Ice axe, Poles, Snowshoes

Felt boots, 46–47; *ill.* 46
First aid, 74–77
Footgear, 45–47; *ill.* 46
Frostbite, 79

Games, 96–99. *See also* Racing
Green Mountain modified bearpaw (snowshoe style), 17–19, 32, 56, 116; *ill.* 18, 23
Group travel, 66–70
Grouse, 67; *ill.* 68
Gut, 30–31. *See also* Babiche

Headgear, 48–49
Heel control binding, 40; *ill.* 40
Hill climbing technique, 58–63; *ill.* 59, 61
Horse, snowshoes for, 24; *ill.* 24
Huron Indians, 6
Hypothermia, 74–76

Ice axe, 53
Ice travel technique, 65–66
Indians, 2, 6; *ill.* 4
Inner tube (rubber) binding, 40–44; *ill.* 42, 43
International Snowshoer's Committee, 9

Jigs, for making snowshoes, 122–123; *ill.* 122, 123

Kits, snowshoe, 135

Lacing. *See* Babiche, Neoprene, Nylon
Lacing patterns, 30–31, 127–135; *ill.*
   132, 133
Lamp wick binding, 34
Layering principle (clothing), 45–50
Leadership, 68–70, 71

Maine (snowshoe style), 17, 20; *ill.* 20
Making snowshoes, 111–136; *ill.* 115,
   118, 119, 120, 122, 123, 125, 128,
   129, 130, 132, 133, 134. *See also*
   Babiche, Jigs, Lacing patterns,
   Manufacture, commercial; Steamer
Manufacture, commercial, 28–33. *See
   also* Making snowshoes
Manufacturers, 140–146
Michigan (snowshoe style), 17, 20, 116;
   ill. 20
Military snowshoes, 2, 6, 19, 34–37;
   ill. 5
Mittens, 49
Moccasins, 45–46; *ill.* 46
Montreal Snow Shoe Club, 8; *ill.* 10

Neoprene lacing, 30–31. *See also*
   Babiche
Northfield, Vermont, 11, 109
Nylon lacing, 31. *See also* Babiche
Nylon strap binding, 34; *ill.* 35

Ojibwa (snowshoe style), 19, 123–134;
   ill. 20, 123, 128, 129, 130, 132,
   133, 134
Outings, 11–14; *ill.* 15. *See also*
   Games, Racing

Pants, 48
Parkas, 48
Pickerel (snowshoe style), 19
Plastic snowshoes, 20, 23; *ill.* 20, 23
Poles, 53, 62–63; *ill.* 52, 62

Quin-zhee, 93–94

Racing, 100–110, 111; *ill.* 101, 103,
   104, 105, 107
Rawhide lacing, 30–31. *See also*
   Babiche

Reindeer hide boots, 44
Repairs, of snowshoes, 54–55,
   71–72; *ill.* 71
Rescue techniques, 84–91; *ill.* 90

Siwash binding, 65
Size guide, 32
Skis, 6, 28
Sleds, 89–91; *ill.* 90
Smoke, 94
Snowmobile boots, 46; *ill.* 46
Snowmobiles, 16, 85
Snowshoe construction, 28–33,
   111–136; *ill.* 115, 118, 119, 120,
   122, 123, 125, 128, 129, 130, 132,
   133, 134
Snowshoe selection, 17–33; *ill.* 18, 20,
   22, 23
Snowshoe styles. *See* Alaskan,
   Algonquin, Bearpaw, Beavertail,
   Green Mountain modified
   bearpaw, Maine, Michigan,
   Ojibwa, Pickerel, Trail, Westover.
   See also Kits, Plastic snowshoes
Snowshoeing. *See* Techniques
Socks, 47
Squaw hitch binding, 38–40; *ill.* 41
Steamer, 124; *ill.* 119, 125
Stoves, 94
Survival techniques, 71–76, 84–91;
   ill. 90
Swiss army snowshoes, *ill.* 26

Techniques, 56–70
Tents, 94
Tobaggan camp, 92–93
Toe hole, 31
Trail (snowshoe style), 19; *ill.* 20
Trail breaking, 63, 89–90
Traversing, 59; *ill.* 57, 59
Truger (snowshoe style), 28
Tuque, 48–49
Turning techniques, 59–60

Uniforms, 8; *ill.* 7, 10
United States Snowshoe Association,
   9–11, 100
Uphill travel, 58–60; *ill.* 59

Varnish, 33, 133
Variations, 24–28; *ill.* 25, 26, 27

Water treatment, 95
Weight and size, 32–33
Westover modified bearpaw (snowshoe style), 17, 32, 56

Whales (snowshoe style), 28
Whippers-in, 12, 69
Winter camp, 92–95
Wood, for snowshoes, 114–117, 136; *ill.* 115
Wooden (board) snowshoes, 24–29; *ill.* 25, 26